THE IMPERIAL

CONTEXT AND COMMENTARY

Series Editor: ARTHUR POLLARD

Published

J. A. V. Chapple
SCIENCE AND LITERATURE IN THE
NINETEENTH CENTURY

J. A. Downie
TO SETTLE THE SUCCESSION OF THE STATE

C. C. Eldridge
THE IMPERIAL EXPERIENCE

Dominic Hibberd
THE FIRST WORLD WAR

Pamela Horn
LIFE AND LABOUR IN RURAL ENGLAND,
1760–1850

Elisabeth Jay
FAITH AND DOUBT IN VICTORIAN BRITAIN

Norman Page
THE THIRTIES IN BRITAIN

Stephen Prickett
ENGLAND AND THE FRENCH REVOLUTION

Alan and Dorothy Shelston
THE INDUSTRIAL CITY

Robin Headlam Wells
SHAKESPEARE, POLITICS AND THE STATE

THE IMPERIAL EXPERIENCE

From Carlyle to Forster

C. C. Eldridge

First published 1996 by
MACMILLAN PRESS LTD
Houndmills, Basingstoke, Hampshire RG21 6XS
and London
Companies and representatives
throughout the world

ISBN 0-333-43775-6 hardcover
ISBN 0-333-43776-4 paperback

A catalogue record for this book is available
from the British Library.

10 9 8 7 6 5 4 3 2 1
05 04 03 02 01 00 99 98 97 96

Typeset by Pure Tech India Ltd, Pondicherry

Printed in Hong Kong

THERE IS A BRITISH EMPIRE

FOREIGNERS

PLEASE TAKE NOTICE AND KEEP

OFF IT

C. R. L. Fletcher and R. Kipling,
A History of England (1911)

To Ruth

Contents

List of Plates

Editor's Preface

J. H. Plumb has said that 'the aim of (the historian) is to understand men both as individuals and in their social relationships in time. "Social" embraces all of man's activities – economic, religious, political, artistic, legal, military, scientific – everything, indeed, that affects the life of mankind.' Literature is itself similarly comprehensive. From Terence onwards writers have embraced his dictum that all things human are their concern.

It is the aim of this series to trace the interweavings of history and literature, to show by judicious quotation and commentary how those actually working within the various fields of human activity influenced and were influenced by those who were writing the novels, poems and plays within the several periods. An attempt has been made to show the special contribution that such writers make to the understanding of their times by virtue of their peculiar imaginative 'feel' for their subjects and the intensely personal angle from which they observe the historical phenomena that provide their inspiration and come within their creative vision. In its turn the historical evidence, besides and beyond its intrinsic importance, serves to 'place' the imaginative testimony of the writers.

The authors of the several volumes in this series have sought to intermingle history and literature in the conviction that the study of each is enhanced thereby. They have been free to adopt their own approach within the broad general pattern of the series. The topics themselves have sometimes also a particular slant and emphasis. Commentary, for instance, has had to be more detailed in\some cases than in others. All the contributors to the series are at one, however, in the belief (at a time when some critics would not only divorce texts from their periods but even from their authors) that literature is the creation of actual men and women, actually living in an identifiable set of historical circumstances, themselves both the creatures and the creators of their times.

ARTHUR POLLARD

Author's Preface

This volume is intended as an introductory text for those studying the literature and history of the British empire during the nineteenth and early twentieth centuries. As such, it builds on the work and pioneering efforts of a multitude of historians and literary specialists too numerous to acknowledge. The book is also the product of an attempt to provide a genuinely interdisciplinary course on 'Images of Empire', extending well beyond the realm of literature, for a Victorian Studies degree scheme. Much is therefore owed to the tolerance and cooperation of colleagues across the disciplines, as well as the stimulus of teaching several generations of enquiring and critical students. Their contribution has been invaluable.

When the course began in the late 1970s, there was no suitable textbook covering so broad a field. This was soon remedied with the appearance of John MacKenzie's *Propaganda and Empire* (1984) and the launching of the 'Studies in Imperialism' series by Manchester University Press whose contributors have so advanced our understanding of cultural imperialism. This book has benefited greatly from their efforts and example, though its faults and omissions remain entirely my own.

In other respects, the book is both a product of the renewed interest amongst literary specialists in what used to be called the 'literature of imperialism' and a reaction to some recent developments in the literary study of that subject. I refer not simply to the understandable tendency to concentrate on élite texts, as though the works of Forster and Orwell relating to empire can be regarded as representative of the writing and thinking of the inter-war period, nor to the heavy concentration on political correctness and the invention of jargon, but to the tendency in much recent colonial discourse analysis to divorce literary texts from the conditions and circumstances in which they were produced.

As a result, imperialism has frequently been turned into a static, vague and generalised concept, shorn of its complexities and ambiguities, isolated from historical events, the subtleties of economic and political relationships, and the changing intellectual climate of the day. The founders of Orientalist Studies have suffered in a similar way: scholars who admired and sympathised with all things Indian, and whose sole wish was to preserve them, are now accused of having developed a destructive weapon aimed at perpetuating Western intellectual dominance and imperial rule. Such misreadings of the historical record not only confuse intention and effect, but force late twentieth-century perceptions and susceptibilities onto nineteenth-century words and actions. As a consequence, hostile moral verdicts have been cast on whole previous generations. Historians, viewing such interpretations as ahistorical, have generally avoided participation in such disputes.

This volume, then, in its attempt to place the imaginative literature of the British imperial experience firmly within a broad chronological framework, will no doubt be viewed by some as old fashioned in its attempt to establish a relationship between ideas, intellectual movements and events. It is nevertheless hoped that it will be of use, especially to the student, in placing the literature of the day in its proper social, economic and political context and shifting intellectual climate, emphasising as it does the intermingling of pro-empire and anti-empire themes, changing perceptions of the role and function of empire, and the divergences, and striking convergences, of élite and popular culture.

My many debts to historians and literary commentators will be obvious from the text. In writing the book, I would particularly like to single out Kathy Miles and Robert Ford, of the inter-library loan service of the University of Wales, Lampeter, for their efficient service, unfailing courtesy and willingness to help with bibliographical checks. Like all contributors to this series, I have also benefited greatly from the wise counsel and continued encouragement of the General Editor, Arthur Pollard, who has coaxed a text from this somewhat hesitant contributor to a literary series. My thanks also go to a succession of editors at the publishers for their patience and understanding when events diverted me into more mundane affairs.

C. C. ELDRIDGE

Introduction

> From my heart, I thank my beloved people. May God bless them.

With these words, telegraphed around the world on 22 June 1897, Queen Victoria thanked the peoples of her empire on the occasion of her Diamond Jubilee. The subjects she addressed constituted a quarter of the world's population, nearly four hundred million people who occupied more than eleven million square miles, almost a quarter of the earth's surface. At the end of a day of imperial pageantry the tired but grateful Queen-Empress wrote in her private journal:

> A never-to-be-forgotten day. No one ever, I believe, has met with such an ovation as was given to me, passing through those six miles of streets. The crowds were quite indescribable and their enthusiasm truly marvellous and deeply touching [. . . .] Every face seemed to be filled with joy. I was much moved and gratified.

About the same time a more detached observer, the socialist Beatrice Webb, recorded in her diary:

> Imperialism in the air. All classes drunk with sightseeing and hysterical loyalty.

> Entry, 28 June 1897, *The Diary of Beatrice Webb. Vol. 2: 1892–1895* (1983), edited by J. & N. MacKenzie, p. 118

By the end of the nineteenth century the Queen and her empire had become synonymous.

It had been an extraordinary day. It was an extraordinary time. The somewhat bellicose outpouring of British pride, chauvinism and cultural arrogance, seen again during the

Fashoda crisis with France in 1898 and in the heady demonstrations of patriotic fervour and near-hysteria which accompanied the reliefs of Kimberley, Ladysmith and
Mafeking during the Boer War, were but louder and cruder
versions of earlier bouts of popular excitement. In the 1850s
and 1860s, the Indian Mutiny, the Morant Bay rebellion and
the prosecution of Governor Eyre had created a tremendous
stir. In 1877–8, a surge of public interest in the Eastern
Question added the word 'jingoism' to the English language.
Much public excitement had also been aroused by the deaths
of Dr Livingstone and General Gordon, the charting of the
map of Africa, the Ashanti, Zulu and first Anglo–Boer Wars,
the Jameson Raid, and the various Egyptian campaigns of
1882, 1884–5 and 1896–8. This was the 'Age of the New
Imperialism' when new intellectual and social currents
sought to explain, justify and promote European penetration
of distant areas of the globe.

It was also the period when imperial ideology became part
of the language of patriotism. By the end of the century
intellectual and popular tastes had converged. 'High' culture
and 'popular' culture marched in time to the music of Elgar
and the patriotic songs of the music hall. The Art Establishment and the man-in-the-street admired the military
paintings of Lady Butler. The stories of G. A. Henty, Rider
Haggard and Kipling, and the poetry of Sir Henry Newbolt
and W. E. Henley, were eagerly read. Theories generated by
the proponents of social Darwinism, muscular Christianity
and public school athleticism were equally readily absorbed.
Cadet corps, the Boys' Brigade and the Boy Scouts movements were established for the newly literate and educated
young. New national traditions and hero-worshipping cults
grew up around an imperial matriarch. As the British public
warmed to the exploits narrated by war correspondents, the
sentiments expressed in the 'yellow press' received increasingly widespread endorsement. Commenting on the 'rum-
bustious and stentorian' patriotism of the 1890s, Esmé
Wingfield-Stratford later recalled:

> I can dimly remember the first Jubilee, and the sec-
> ond very clearly indeed; my favourite literature as a
> schoolboy consisted in accounts of future wars from

which, after an agreeably awful slaughter, the British empire would emerge vaster and more imperial than ever [. . .] about patriotism in those empire conscious days there was no doubt or room for doubt. It meant an honest-to-God or Satan – love for your country, right or wrong – not that she ever was wrong, to signify – and loving your country meant shouting, and going all out, and, at need, dying, for that empire on which, as we were constantly reminded, the sun never set. To doubt this, or oppose it in any way, was treason.

Esmé Wingfield-Stratford, *The Foundations of British Patriotism* (1940), p. x

Of course, there were dissenting voices: empire, let alone imperialism, had never been to the liking of all. But it was clearly the dominant ideology. An arch-opponent of the imperial credo commented wryly:

Let's learn to think Imperially,
'Twill smooth our path materially;
Let us reflect on what we gain
By thinking in imperial vein.

Imperial thinking, high and grand,
Induced us to acquire the Rand,
It's given us a party cry
Good when election time is nigh.

It's won us the undying hate
Of every European state
Against whose face we wave our flag
With blessed 'Rule Britannia' brag.

For this we eat, for this we drink,
For this to idiocy we sink,
To bursting points our Budgets swell,
And in our slums gaunt paupers dwell.

> But who to heart would such things take
> When glorious Empire is at stake?
>
> Sir Wilfrid Lawson, 'Learn to Think Imperially',
> (19 January 1904), *Cartoons in Rhyme and Line*
> (1905), p. 24

The late Victorian and Edwardian world-view was assuredly imperial.

The Frontiers of Fear

But all was not as it appeared on the surface. The demonstrations of patriotic fervour were not simply outbursts of national pride and racial arrogance: they were as much the product of deep feelings of insecurity and uncertainty. British pre-eminence in the world had seriously declined. Even before the death of Palmerston in 1865, Great Britain's views on European issues had begun to count for little. Disraeli, it is true, during the Russo–Turkish War and the Congress of Berlin succeeded temporarily in restoring British prestige, but this was soon dented by the disasters accompanying the Zulu and Afghan Wars, the defeat at Majuba Hill in 1881, and the much-publicised failure of the Gladstone government to relieve General Gordon at Khartoum. Bismarck's Germany now dominated the continent. America's shadow was stretching across the Atlantic. Russia was advancing in the Balkans, Central Asia and the Far East. Japan was undergoing a programme of rapid modernisation. In the closing decades of the nineteenth century, the British had to content themselves with a series of cardboard victories against native peoples, mainly in Africa.

Even here Britain did not possess a free hand. As the nations of Europe sought to acquire, maintain or regain political supremacy, the struggle transferred to safer tournament grounds overseas. European disputes became internationalised. Some British commentators began to fear that Britain's ever increasing global responsibilities were in danger of overtaxing British military and naval strength. One prominent Liberal critic warned in 1892:

It is my conviction that we already have as much Empire as the nation can carry. If you give the heart too much work to do by extending the limbs and the frame beyond measure you enfeeble its action, and it succumbs.

> Sir William Harcourt to the Earl of Rosebery,
> 27 September 1892, quoted in A. G. Gardiner,
> *Life of Sir William Harcourt* (1923), Vol. 2, p. 196

After the humiliations of the second Anglo–Boer War, when it had taken the might of the British empire three years to defeat a population approximately half the size of Birmingham, Rudyard Kipling cautioned his compatriots:

> *Let us admit it fairly as a business people should,*
> *We have had no end of a lesson: it will do us no end*
> *of good.*

> Not on a single issue, or in one direction or twain,
> But conclusively, comprehensively, and several
>   times and again,
> Were all our most holy illusions knocked higher
>   than Gilderoy's kite.
> We have had a jolly good lesson, and it serves us
>   jolly well right!

> [. . .]

> It was our fault, and our very great fault – and now
>   we must turn it to use.
> We have forty million reasons for failure, but not a
>   single excuse.
> So the more we work and the less we talk the better
>   results we shall get.
> We have had an Imperial lesson. It may make us an
>   Empire yet!

> R. Kipling, 'The Lesson' (1899–1902), ll. 1–6, 27–30

In 'The Islanders' (1902), Kipling further castigated the 'flannelled fools at the wicket', the 'muddied oafs at the goals' and the general state of military unpreparedness. It comes as no surprise that the British governments of the early twentieth century soon set about reorganising the armed forces, made new arrangements to protect British interests overseas, and began implementing social reforms to improve the lot of the working man who had so frequently been ignominiously rejected as unfit for military service. Empire and social reform became entwined not only in the schemes of Joseph Chamberlain but also in the policies of the Liberal government of 1906 which included the Liberal Imperialists Asquith, Haldane and Grey. National efficiency was the new watchword.

The failure of the British economy to match those of its rivals was an additional cause for concern. Joseph Chamberlain's scheme to create a great imperial federation, designed to ensure Great Britain's survival into the twentieth century as a world power, also had an economic component: the creation of a colonial *zollverein*, a gigantic imperial economic community. For not only had the return to protective tariffs by Great Britain's trading rivals facilitated industrial revolutions in Germany, France, Belgium and the United States, effectively closing large markets to British products, but the home market itself had been invaded by foreign competitors. During the years of the so-called 'Great Depression', the hardship was particularly badly felt. The markets of the non-industrialised world alone remained open. Even that hardened diplomat and cynic, Lord Salisbury, concluded that precautionary claims had to be made to forestall rivals. His political opponent, Lord Rosebery, agreed:

> It is said that our Empire is already large enough and does not need extension. That would be true enough if the world were elastic, but, unfortunately, it is not elastic, and we are engaged at the present moment in the language of mining in 'pegging out claims for the future'. [...] We have to consider what countries must be developed either by ourselves or by some other nation, and we have to remember that it is part of our responsibility and heritage to take care that the world, as far as it can be moulded by us, shall receive the Anglo-Saxon and not another character.

[. . .] We have to look forward beyond the chatter of
platforms and the passions of party to the future of
the race of which we are at present the trustees, and
we should in my opinion grossly fail in the task that
has been laid upon us did we shrink from responsibilities and decline to take our share in a partition of
the world which we have not forced on, but which
has been forced upon us.

> The Earl of Rosebery, speech at the Anniversary
> Banquet of the Royal Colonial Institute,
> 1 March 1893, *The Times*, 2 March 1893

In the 1890s empire became a popular panacea for declining
trade, over-population, growing unemployment and for
securing future greatness.

The Climax of Imperialism

In many ways, the truculent mood of much of the British
public at the turn of the century was a direct response to
these increasingly worrying signs of diplomatic isolation and
industrial and commercial stagnation. The growing coarse-
ness of that society is revealed in an extraordinary poem by
John Davidson, unusual in both its concentration on the
economics of imperialism and in the ruthlessness of its trib-
ute to a successful self-made man, Cecil Rhodes. In the
poem, Heaven is full of the bold and enterprising. Hell,
containing 'the greater part of all the swarthy, all the tawny
tribes', is occupied by the weak and the unadventurous. The
Empire-Builder, however, willingly took the path from
which the altruistic recoiled:

> For me, I clambered into Heaven at once
> And stayed there; joined the warfare of the times
> In corner, trust and syndicate: upheaved
> A furrow, hissing through the angry world,
> A redshot ploughshare in a frozen glebe,
> And reaped my millions long before my prime.
> Then, being English, one of the elect
> Above all folks, within me fate grew strong.

> The authentic mandate of imperial doom
> Undid my simple, immature, design,
> And made me – what! Tenfold a criminal?
> No other name for Hastings, Clive and me!
> I broke your slothful dreams of folded wings,
> Of work achieved and empire circumscribed,
> Dispelled the treacherous flatteries of peace,
> And thrust upon you in your dull despite
> The one thing needful, half a continent
> Of habitable land! The English Hell
> Forever crowds upon the English Heaven.
> Secure your birthright; set the world at nought;
> Confront your fate; regard the naked deed;
> Enlarge your Hell; preserve it in repair;
> Only a splendid Hell keeps Heaven fair.

> John Davidson, *The Testament of an Empire Builder*
> (1902), p. 81

The poem is exceptional in many ways. Such sentiments of aggression and appeals to commit 'naked deeds' did not normally suit the tender British conscience – especially at a time of international criticism of Britain's internment of Boer women and children in 'concentration' camps and allegations concerning 'methods of barbarism' adopted by Kitchener in the conduct of that war. Appeals to morality, to 'Take up the White Man's Burden', were much more to the public's liking.

But Great Britain's international problems (whatever fears they gave rise to) were clearly not sufficient to instil British imperialism with all the mysticism of a religious faith. This element, initially provided by philanthropists, anti-slavers and missionary societies, was rapidly reinforced by highly publicised theories concerning British racial and cultural superiority. Commerce, Christianity and the civilization of the less fortunate peoples of the world joined forces in promoting Great Britain's national mission. By the end of the nineteenth century, imperial expansion had acquired a high moral purpose. Joseph Chamberlain claimed:

> We feel now that our rule over these territories can
> only be justified if we can show that it adds to the

happiness and prosperity of the people, and I maintain that our rule does, and has, brought security and peace and comparative prosperity to countries that have never known these blessings before.

In carrying out this work of civilization we are fulfilling what I believe to be our national mission, and we are finding scope for the exercise of those faculties and qualities which have made of us a great governing race. I do not say that our success has been perfect in every case, I do not say that all our methods have been beyond reproach; but I do say that in almost every instance in which the rule of the Queen has been established and the great *Pax Britannica* has been enforced, there has come with it a greater security to life and property, and a material improvement in the condition of the bulk of the population [. . . .] You cannot have omelettes without breaking eggs; you cannot destroy the practices of barbarism, of slavery, of superstition which for centuries have desolated the interior of Africa, without the use of force; but if you will fairly contrast the gain to humanity with the price for which we are bound to pay for it, I think that you may well rejoice [. . . .] Great is the task, great is the responsibility, but great is the honour; and I am convinced that the conscience and the spirit of the country will rise to the height of its obligations, and that we shall have the strength to fulfil the mission which our history and our national character have imposed upon us.

> Joseph Chamberlain, speech at the Royal Colonial Institute, 31 March 1897, quoted in G. Bennett (ed.), *The Concept of Empire: Burke to Attlee, 1774–1947* (1967), pp. 318–19

This was the spirit of empire which took the British public by storm in the year of Queen Victoria's Diamond Jubilee. In part created by politicians, philanthropists, missionary societies, the business world and the press, it was also the creation of intellectuals, academics, the artistic and the literary fraternity, as this book will attempt to show. With the spread of literacy in the late nineteenth century the written word had a greater impact on society than ever before. The age of Disraeli, Gladstone, Salisbury, Rosebery and Chamberlain, the era of Henty, Haggard, Kipling, Newbolt, Conrad and Buchan, also saw the publication of Sir Charles Dilke's *Greater Britain* (1868), Charles Darwin's *Descent of Man* (1871), Sir John Seeley's *The Expansion of England* (1883), C. H. Pearson's *National Life and Character* (1893), Benjamin Kidd's *Social Evolution* (1894) and J. A. Cramb's *Reflections on the Origins and Destiny of Imperial Britain* (1900). For once, most of the intelligentsia, the Establishment, the churches, the military, the aristocracy, the middle classes and, it is said, the working classes, were united in professing a faith in empire which bordered on the fanatical. During these years, the late 1890s especially, the majority of the British public succumbed to an imperial fervour the like of which has never since been seen.

The Wider Context

Such an unusual meeting of minds was short-lived. For some, the Anglo–Boer War knocked the gilt off the Victorian age. The publication in 1902 of J. A. Hobson's *Imperialism, A Study* certainly ensured that thereafter 'imperialism' became a term of abuse in the international vocabulary. For others, it was the First World War that led to the rejection of militarist nationalism and imperialist sentiment alike. Mindless patriotism and empty-headed jingoism perished in the mud of Flanders. By 1921, the year the British empire reached its widest expanse, most of the elements supporting empire at the end of the previous century had largely disappeared from British society. The music hall quickly lost popularity and faded from the scene. Fashions changed in art and Lady Butler's submission to the Royal Academy was rejected in 1924. Edward Elgar grew to dislike the more patriotic of his compositions, especially the bombast of 'Land of Hope and Glory'. Kipling's verse lost favour and went through a prolonged period of unpopularity. Indeed, it was in the literary sphere that intellectual distaste for imperialism became most apparent: the writings of Robert Graves, Siegfried Sassoon, R. C. Sherriff and H. G. Wells were far different in content and tone from those of their near contemporaries. The Empire Exhibition at Wembley in 1924 was mocked by P. G. Wodehouse and Noel Coward ('I've brought you to see the wonders of the Empire and all you want to do is to go on the dodgems'). Above all, the publication of E. M. Forster's widely acclaimed and highly critical *A Passage to India* (1924) was thought to mark a new literary era as the 'literature of imperialism' followed the New Imperialism into oblivion.

But the neat division of literature and history into clear-cut and contrasting phases is rarely satisfactory and never particularly enlightening. Throughout the nineteenth and twentieth centuries there was much continuity in thought, action and beliefs. The early and mid-Victorian years, for example, witnessed a rapid expansion of empire, especially in India where the great annexations were all accomplished before the Indian Mutiny in 1857. During the years 1815–65, the British empire expanded by roughly just under 100 000 square miles per annum. During the period 1865–1914, it expanded by just over 100 000 square miles per annum. And the prizes gained late in the century were frequently much less valuable than earlier acquisitions. Nor was the empire absent from the literature of the period pre-1880 – as the readers of Carlyle, Trollope, Thackeray, Tennyson, Dickens, Ballantyne, Marryat and even Austen and Gaskell well know.

Similarly, the period after the First World War did not witness the immediate demise of all things appertaining to empire. Far from losing its *raison d'être* in the inter-war and post-Second World War years, the empire became economically more significant. Even after the loss of the Indian lynchpin in 1947, attempts were made to salvage what remained in such last-ditch efforts as the Federation of the Rhodesias and Nyasaland (1953–63). While some means of popular entertainment, like the music halls, may have quickly disappeared, their propaganda role was taken over by even more effective media such as broadcasting and the cinema: witness the great trilogies in the 1930s by Alexander Korda ('the Kipling of the kinema') – *Sanders of the River* (1935), *The Drum* (1938), *The Four Feathers* (1939) – and by Michael Balcon – *Rhodes of Africa* (1936), *The Great Barrier* (1936),

King Solomon's Mines (1937) – all redolent of the attitudes of the 1890s. The same values and beliefs continued to be peddled in the youth movements, school texts, popular comics, and in the writings of Edgar Wallace, John Buchan, W. E. Johns (of Biggles fame) and 'Sapper' (Cyril McNeile). According to John Julius Norwich, in the thirties:

> Empire was all around us, celebrated on our biscuit tins, chronicled on our cigarette cards, part of the fabric of our lives. We were all imperialists then.
>
> John Julius Norwich, *The Radio Three Magazine*, November 1982, p. 42

The same patriotic attitudes, reverence for royalty, racial ideas, and nineteenth-century world-view were still being preached in the school history and geography textbooks of the 1950s. The empire continued to appear centre stage in the novels of Joyce Cary, Graham Greene, John Masters and Doris Lessing. Little wonder, then, that the British seem to have had a long-running post-imperial identity crisis, occasionally indulging in waves of imperial nostalgia in which films, television, novels (notably those of Paul Scott) and exhibitions have figured prominently. Not surprisingly, these facets of the English character have tended to surface at times of crisis, the Falklands War of 1982 and, to a lesser extent, the more recent Gulf War being obvious examples. In fact, the Falklands War was a virtual re-run of one of the 'little wars' of Queen Victoria's reign – the colonial crisis overseas, the hurried despatch of an expeditionary force, the British public agog for news, the same 'John Bull spirit', the jingoistic press, the cheering crowds on the return of the troops, the award of medals, the victory parades and services of thanksgiving. As economic and social problems at home were temporarily swept aside, the Thatcher government enjoyed an election victory reminiscent of the 'Khaki election' of 1900. Finally, the war was followed by the traditional rushing into print as publishers, journalists, popular writers and the visual artists of the 1980s sought to profit from the British public's seemingly unquenchable thirst for information and titillation. The 'spectatorial passion' J. A. Hobson had castigated so sharply in his *Psychology of Jingoism* (1901) was still a potent force 80 years later.

Clearly, many of the beliefs and assumptions which had underpinned imperial ideology continued to maintain their hold on the British character and traditions long after the Second World War. For these reasons, even though the four decades which straddle the turn of the century no longer stand out in such stark contrast, this period has continued to fascinate historians and literary specialists alike. Neither before nor since has the majority of the British people, of whatever class or political persuasion, been so united in expressing faith in empire and the British right to rule. The convergence of the interests of the Establishment and the masses, of intellectual and popular ideas, was remarkable. Never since has the British public been so saturated by imperial ideology. Put simply, the very state of being English embodied such high moral and heroic values that the possession of empire needed no further justification.

These were indeed extraordinary years. The literature of the age both reflected and legitimised, popularised and romanticised, the dominant ideology of the day. It is with the contribution of this literature to the revival of an expansionist spirit, the creation of an imperial ethos, and in the formation of attitudes towards the government and administation of empire – in constructing and perpetuating a British world-view – that this volume is concerned.

Definitions: Imperialism, Imperialists and Imperial Ideology

> Imperialism! Hang the word! It buzzes in my noddle
> Like bumble-bees in clover time. The talk on't's
>   mostly twaddle;
> Yet one would like to fix the thing, as farmer nail up
>   vermin;
> Lots o' big words collapse, like blobs, if their sense
>   you once determine.

> Punch, 23 November 1878, p. 233

During the late 1870s three new terms entered the popular political vocabulary of the day: 'imperialism', 'jingoism' and 'Beaconsfieldism'. Each was used in relation to Disraeli's conduct of foreign and imperial affairs and, by the general election of 1880, all three had become damaging political smear-words. Of the three 'imperialism' was the most hotly debated and the most reviled.

'Imperialism' had first entered the English language in the 1840s when it was used to describe the aims of the *parti impérialiste* in France which sought to revive the glories of the Napoleonic era. Since 1852 it had been associated with the Second Empire of Napoleon III and referred specifically to a government which glorified its leader, practised despotic rule at home, indulged in ostentatious military display, sought popular acclamation, and embarked on aggressive policies overseas. The first application to British domestic politics came during the acrimonious debates on the Royal Titles Bill creating the Queen 'Empress of India'. Such a title, with its continental associations, its despotic and Caesarist connotations implying a status above the law, was not well received. *Punch* urged:

> Lay the imperial style apart;
> Leave it to the lords of legions:
> Queen in every English heart,
> Be thou Queen in Eastern regions.
> Keep thy style and state serene –
> Who so great as India's Queen?
>
> *Punch*, 26 February 1876, p. 74

The Times stigmatised the new title as 'threatening the Crown with the degradation of a tawdry Imperialism' (17 March 1876). *The Spectator* commented:

> It is not easy to realise that such a policy as that of the 'Imperialists', as they are called on the Continent, should have, we will not say any root, but even any possibility of root, in these islands. Yet it is evident that Mr. Disraeli conceived very early in his career the notion that such a policy, – a policy which

should magnify the Crown on the one hand, and the wishes of the masses on the other, and should make light of the constitutional limitations on either, – was still possible in Europe, and might even have a chance in England [. . . .]

The Spectator, 8 April 1876, p. 457

Disraeli's subsequent actions in the Eastern Question led to further denunciations of government policy. Robert Lowe, the only man in the House of Commons whose hand Disraeli vowed he would never shake, attacked his old enemy with customary venom:

What does *Imperialism* mean? It means the assertion of absolute force over others. [...] If we can, by abating somewhat of our extreme right, or even by larger concessions, avert the calamities of war, that is utterly repugnant to Imperialism. But if by the menace of overbearing force we can coerce a weaker state to bow before our will, or if, better still, we can by a demonstration of actual force attain the same object, or, best of all, if we can conquer our adversary in open fight, and impose our own conditions at the bayonet's point, then, as Dryden sings, 'these are imperial arts and worthy thee'. It does not follow that the strongest party is always in the wrong, but the triumph of Imperialism is most complete when power is most clearly manifested; and of course the victory is doubled when the victory is not only over weakness but over right.

R. Lowe, 'Imperialism', *Fortnightly Review* (1878), Vol. 24, pp. 458–9

By 1880, following the Zulu and third Afghan Wars, both of which began disastrously for the British, such attacks had hit their mark and the Disraeli government was decisively defeated at the polls. *The Times* (11 March 1880) recorded that the word 'imperialism' had been 'invented to stamp Lord Beaconsfield's supposed designs with popular reprobation'. Since imperialism did not enter the British political lexicon until the late 1870s, this creates a number of problems for our study. Of course, it does not imply that before this time the activities described by the newly-adopted word did not exist. Imperialism, in this respect, is as old as the hills. But the word has too often been defined in the sense of the 'new' imperialism – belligerent expansionism, authoritarian government and jingoism – and the absence of these factors used to infer the absence of imperialism. Thus the years from 1815 to 1870, when external pressures for territorial expansion were few, were once dubbed an era of indifference to empire, even of 'anti-imperialism'. In this light, the writings of someone like Thomas Carlyle can only be viewed as idiosyncratic, those of a prophet before his time. Failure to define terms with sufficient precision leads only to confusion.

The definition of 'imperialism' has bedevilled historical and literary studies. Contemporaries were equally confused. For some the term was one of opprobrium; others proudly declared themselves to be imperialists, seeing the British empire as the greatest instrument for good that the world had ever seen. An influential section of the Liberal party were known as Liberal Imperialists. These imperialists were not 'jingoists'. They were opponents of what J. R. Seeley called the 'bombastic' school of imperialism. Nor was 'territory for territory's sake' ever a dictum subscribed to by any British government. Even for the late Victorians annexation remained a last resort.

How then should the imperialism of the Victorian and Edwardian years be assessed? The amount of imperialism detected will be dependent on the definition adopted: whether pride in empire and continued justification of dominion overseas be sufficient to qualify, or whether it is necessary to show a continuing policy of aggressive expansionism in operation. If the latter approach is followed, given the economic and political background to the early and mid-Victorian years, comparatively few cases of imperialism will be found. Even the late Victorians may be viewed as reluctant imperialists. If the wider view is taken, however, the whole Victorian age, and the post-world-war period, appear unmistakeably imperialist in tone. As Gladstone, the chief denouncer of imperial excesses, admitted:

The sentiment of empire may be called innate in every Briton. If there are exceptions, they are like those of men born blind or lame among us. It is part of our patrimony: born with our birth, dying only with our death; incorporating itself in the first elements of our knowledge, and interwoven with all our habits of mental action upon public affairs. It is a portion of our national stock, which has never been deficient [. . . .]

> W. E. Gladstone, 'England's Mission', *Nineteenth Century* (1878), Vol. 4, p. 569

Although he was opposed to both the extension of territory and to 'Bosnian submissions', he had an equally firm belief in the benefits to be gained from British rule and the 'capital demand upon the national honour' that such a trust entailed. He, too, believed that England had a mission to fulfil. Perhaps Gladstone summed up his views best (and showed how the use of words can confound understanding) when he stated:

While we are opposed to imperialism, we are devoted to empire.

> Speech at Leeds, 7 October 1881, quoted in P. Magnus, *Gladstone, a Biography* (London, 1954), p. 287

Today, there is still no universally agreed definition of 'imperialism', as a glance at the *Oxford English Dictionary* and the *Soviet Dictionary of Foreign Words* quickly reveals. Most modern writers tend to use the term in one of four different senses – and it is often this confusion which muddles discussion. Marxists, in general, apply the term to a specific stage in the development of capitalism, the so-called 'last' or 'highest' stage. Non-Marxists tend to use it in two different senses: some limit its use to the *formal* establishment of political control over weaker states through the creation of colonies and protectorates (painting the world map red, blue, green and yellow); others broaden the meaning to include the *informal* exercise of cultural and economic dominance (the exploitation of economic advantages by technologically advanced countries at the expense of non-industrial societies). Some would even widen the definition to include relationships within Europe, the United States and the United Kingdom (the treatment of the Irish, the Scots and the Welsh by their more powerful neighbour). The fourth main sense concerns the ideology or range of ideological positions which supported and enabled the establishment and spread of imperial rule – 'that greater pride in Empire' as Rosebery put it, 'which is called Imperialism and is a larger patriotism'.

In this volume, the term **imperialism** will be used to describe the disposition of one nation or people to establish and maintain rule or control over another nation or people, whether in a political, economic or cultural sense. The supporters of such a cause, whether or not they were jingoists or expansionists, will be described as **imperialists**. As regards the 'larger patriotism':

> By its fruits ye shall know it. It is a spirit, an attitude of mind, an unconquerable hope [. . .] It is a sense of the destiny of England. It is the wider patriotism which conceives our people as a race and not as a chance community.
>
> J. Buchan, *A Lodge in the Wilderness*
> (London, 1906), p. 28.

> Imperialism is above all to all who share it a form of passionate feeling; it is a political religion, for it is a public spirit touched with emotion.
>
> A. V. Dicey, *Lectures on the Relation Between Law and Public Opinion in England During the Nineteenth Century* (2nd edn, London, 1914), p. 45

This 'emotion' or 'faith' will be called the **imperial idea** and the cluster of impulses which constituted the new type of aggressive patriotism – monarchism, militarism, the worship of national heroes, the cult of personality, racial ideas associated with social Darwinism – will be termed **imperial**

ideology. Hopefully, such definitions will help to avoid confusion. They should also permit the elements of continuity
and change to be properly highlighted.

1 The Revival of the Imperial Spirit

England cannot afford to be little. She must be what she is, or nothing [. . . .]

Sir, England is the parent of many flourishing colonies – one of them is become an empire among the most powerful in the world. In every quarter of the globe we have planted the seeds of freedom, civilization and Christianity. To every quarter of the globe we have carried the language, the free institutions, the system of laws, which prevail in this country; – in every quarter they are fructifying and making progress; and if it be said by some selfish calculator, that we have done all this at the expense of sacrifices which we ought not to have made, my answer is, – in spite of these sacrifices, we are still the first and happiest people in the old world; and, whilst this is our lot, let us rejoice rather in that rich harvest of glory, which must belong to a nation that has laid the foundation of similar happiness and prosperity to other nations, kindred in blood, in habits, and in feelings to ourselves.

William Huskisson, House of Commons, 2 May 1828, *Speeches* (1831), Vol. 3, pp. 286–7

Such expressions of a sense of mission, of obligations incurred and responsibilities to be shouldered, as well as outright pride in British achievements overseas, were constantly made throughout the nineteenth century. In 1839, Thomas Carlyle asserted:

To the English people in World History, there have been, shall I prophesy, two grand tasks assigned? Huge-looming through the dim tumult of the always incommensurable Present Time, outlines of two tasks disclose themselves: the grand industrial task of conquering some half or more of this Terraqueous Planet for the use of man; then secondly, the grand Constitutional task of sharing, in some pacific endurable manner, the fruit of said conquest, and showing how it might be done.

T. Carlyle, *Chartism* (1839), Chapter VIII, p. 214

The *Edinburgh Review* explained:

It is a noble work to plant the foot of England and extend her sceptre by the banks of streams unnamed, and over regions yet unknown – and to conquer, not by the tyrannous subjugation of inferior races, but by the victories of mind over brute matter and blind mechanical obstacles. A yet nobler work it is to diffuse over a new created world the laws of Alfred, the language of Shakespeare, and the Christian religion, the last great heritage of man.

Edinburgh Review (1850), Vol. 41, p. 61

The custodians of empire in the early Victorian age emphasised the sense of duty, responsibility and self-sacrifice. Earl Grey, when defending his record as Colonial Secretary during the years 1846–52, stated:

I conceive that, by the acquisition of its Colonial dominions, the Nation has incurred a responsibility of the highest kind, which it is not at liberty to throw off. The authority of the British Crown is at this moment the most powerful instrument, under Providence, of maintaining peace and order in many extensive regions of the earth, and thereby assists in diffusing amongst millions of the human race, the blessings of Christianity and civilization.

Earl Grey, *The Colonial Policy of Lord John Russell's Administration* (1853), Vol. 1, p. 14

Similar sentiments were repeated and emphasised by a later Colonial Secretary, the Earl of Carnarvon, when addressing the Philosophical Institution in Edinburgh in 1878:

> If we turn to that far larger empire over our native fellow-subjects of which I have spoken, the limits expand and the proportions rise till there forms itself a picture so vast and noble that the mind loses itself in the contemplation of what might be under the benificent rule of Great Britain [. . . .] There we have races struggling to emerge into civilization, to whom emancipation from servitude is but the foretaste of the far higher law of liberty and progress to which they may yet attain; and vast populations like those of India sitting like children in the shadow of doubt and poverty and sorrow, yet looking up to us for guidance and for help. To them it is our part to give wise laws, good government, and a well ordered finance, which is the foundation of good things in human communities; it is ours to supply them with a system where the humblest may enjoy freedom from oppression and wrong equally with the greatest; where the light of religion and morality can penetrate into the darkest dwelling places. This is the real fulfilment of our duties; this, again, I say, is the true strength and meaning of imperialism.

> Earl of Carnarvon, 'Imperial Administration',
> *Fortnightly Review* (December, 1878), Vol. 24, pp. 763–4

The imperial idea was clearly present throughout the whole of the nineteenth century.

However, the atmosphere of the early and mid-Victorian years, before the full panoply of imperial ideology came into existence, was very different from that of the age of the New Imperialism. International economic and political conditions were entirely different and British attention focused on evangelical and humanitarian issues, the consolidation (rather than the extension) of the empire, on the colonies of British settlement rather than the tropics, and on the restructuring of the imperial relationship. Imperial ideology had yet to become embedded in British patriotism.

It is possible to trace the evolution of the imperial idea in Tennyson's political poems. For example, to the opening stanzas of 'Hail Briton':

> Hail Briton! in whatever zone
>   Binds the broad earth beneath the blue,
>   In ancient season or in new,
> No bolder front than thine is shown:
>
> Not for the wide sail-wandered tides
>   That ever round thee come and go –
>   The many ships of war that blow
> The battle from their oaken sides –
>
> Not for a power, that knows not check,
>   To spread and float an ermined pall
>   Of Empire, from the ruined wall
> Of royal Delhi to Quebec –

> Lord Tennyson, 'Hail Briton!' (1833), ll. 1–12

Tennyson later added:

> But that in righteousness thy power
>   Doth stand, thine empire on thy word –
>   In thee no traitor voice be heard
> Whatever danger threats the hour!
>
> God keep thee strong as thou art free,
>   Free in the freedom of His law,
>   And brave all wrong to overawe,
> Strong in the strength of unity!
>
> Symbol of loyal brotherhood!
>   Lo, brother-hands shall raise the walls
>   Of these their own Imperial Halls
> And toil within for brothers' good.
>
>   God bless our work!
>   God save our Empress-Queen!

> Harvard Manuscripts, Loosepaper 74 (1886), ll. 13–26,
>   cited in *The Poems of Tennyson* (1987), edited by
>   C. Ricks, Vol. 1, p. 522

Tennyson's frequent revision of his political poems, adding a more explicit imperial dimension in the years post-1870, provides an interesting commentary on developing political attitudes towards empire during the early and mid-Victorian years.

It is also illuminating to trace the role of empire in the novels of the period. Too often has discussion been confined to the writings of a handful of late Victorians and Edwardians. Because tub-thumping jingoism was absent from the earlier years, it has frequently been assumed that little interest was shown in the growing empire. This is far from true. Its presence can be detected even in the serious domestic novels of the age. Sometimes, admittedly, it merely provided background colour or light relief, a convenient reason for the entry or exit of characters, a place for banishment or renewal, a utopia where even the unfortunate might prosper. In other novels, however, it plays a much more central role. Some writers contributed directly to discussions of the main imperial problems of the day.

India, for example, intrudes on the domestic novels of Jane Austen (*Sense and Sensibility*), Charlotte Brontë (*Jane Eyre*) and Elizabeth Gaskell (*Cranford*), as well as, more obviously, in the novels of William Makepeace Thackeray (*Vanity Fair*, *Pendennis*, *The Newcomes* and *The Tremendous Adventures of Major Gahagan*). The West Indian connection is also present in *Mansfield Park* and *Jane Eyre*. Australasia looms large in the writings of Dickens (*Great Expectations*, *David Copperfield* and 'The Convict's Return' in *Pickwick Papers*), Edward Bulwer-Lytton (*The Caxtons*), Trollope (*The Three Clerks*, *John Caldigate* and 'Harry Heathcote of Gangoil' in *The Graphic*, 1873), Henry Kingsley (*The Recollections of Geoffrey Hamlyn*, *The Hillyers and the Burtons*), Charles Reade (*It Is Never Too Late to Mend*), and Samuel Butler (*Erewhon*). In addition, Philip Meadows Taylor, the greatest Anglo-Indian writer before Kipling, wrote perceptively about thuggee (*Confessions of a Thug*) and the Indian Mutiny (*Seeta*). In fact, the Mutiny spawned a whole series of lesser novels: George Lawrence's *Maurice Dering*, James Grant's *First Love and Last Love: A Tale of the Indian Mutiny*, Henry Kingsley's *Stretton* and Sir George Chesney's *The Dilemma*. And when the names of Harriet Martineau (*Dawn Island*), R. M. Ballantyne and Captain Marryat are added to this list, and the contribution of Thomas Carlyle and the various publications of Anthony Trollope on the West Indies, Canada, Australia, New Zealand, South Africa and Ireland are recalled, it soon becomes apparent how omnipresent empire was in the literature of the early and mid-Victorian years. The absence of jingoism and belligerent expansionism, and the many discussions about the value and nature of the imperial relationship, were not the result of any general lack of belief in empire: they were more a product of the specific circumstances of the time.

The 'Little England' Era

The British empire suffered two blows in the late eighteenth century: the loss of the American colonies and Adam Smith's celebrated attack on the old colonial system in *An Inquiry into the Nature and Causes of the Wealth of Nations* (1776). The American Revolution led to a widespread assumption that the rest of the colonies of British settlement would inevitably leave the parental fold when they reached maturity. Mr Seagrave in Marryat's *Masterman Ready* acknowledged this when explaining to Master William why England and other nations were so anxious to have colonies:

> Because they tend so much to the prosperity of the mother country. In their infancy they generally are an expense to her, as they require her care; but as they advance, they are able to repay her by taking her manufactures, and returning for them their own produce; an exchange mutually advantageous, but more so to the mother country than to the colony, as the mother country, assuming to herself the right of supplying all the wants of the colony, has a market for the labour of her own people, without any competition. And here, my boy, you may observe what a parallel there is between a colony and the mother country and a child and its parents. In infancy, the mother country assists and supports the colony as an

infant; as it advances and becomes vigorous, the colony returns the obligation: but the parallel does not end there. As soon as the colony has grown strong and powerful enough to take care of itself, it throws off the yoke of subjection, and declares itself independent; just as a son who has grown up to manhood, leaves his father's house, and takes up a business to gain his own livelihood. This is as certain to be the case, as it is that a bird as soon as it can fly will leave its parent's nest.

Captain Marryat, *Masterman Ready* (1841), p. 116

Unfortunately, Seagrave's economic justification for colonies was rapidly losing its force. After Adam Smith's denunciation of the ramshackle and somewhat haphazardly applied series of commercial and navigation laws known as 'mercantilism', free-trade ideas gradually gained acceptance. As a result, the two main props of the eighteenth-century empire were demolished in the first half of the nineteenth century. Following two minor rebellions in the Canadas in 1837, autocratic government from Whitehall was swept aside as responsible government – the handing over of the control of internal affairs to locally elected assemblies – was introduced into most of the colonies of British settlement in British North America, Australia and New Zealand in the 1840s and 1850s. The same decades witnessed the triumph of the new economic doctrines of free trade.

Since there was no longer any obvious connection between commercial prosperity and the possession of empire, one school of thought (the so-called 'Manchester School') led by Cobden and Bright, viewed colonies as burdens on the British exchequer, especially where defence costs were concerned. Goldwin Smith, Regius Professor of Modern History at Oxford, put the matter squarely:

The time was when the universal prevalence of commercial monopoly made it well worth our while to hold Colonies in dependence for the sake of commanding their trade. But that time is gone. Trade is everywhere free, or becoming free; and this expensive and perilous connection has entirely survived its sole legitimate cause. It is time that we should recognise the change that has come over the world.

We have, in fact, long felt that the Colonies did nothing for us. We now are very naturally beginning to grumble at being put to the expense of doing anything for them. If they are to do nothing for us, and we are to do nothing for them, where is the use of continuing the connexion?

G. Smith, *The Empire* (1863), p. 2

The book was a wholesale indictment of the imperial system.

Accordingly, calls for releasing the colonies of British settlement from the imperial yoke multiplied. In 1859, Anthony Trollope asserted that a state of dependency was not only humiliating, it retarded the growth of the colonies:

We have a noble mission, but we are never content with it. It is not enough for us to beget nations, civilize countries, and instruct in truth and knowledge the dominant races of the coming ages. All this will not suffice unless also we can maintain a king over them! What is it to us, or even to them, who may be their king or ruler – or, to speak with a nearer approach to sense, from what source they may be governed – so long as they be happy, prosperous, and good? And yet there are men mad enough to regret the United States! Many men are mad enough to look forward with anything but composure to the inevitable, happily inevitable day, when Australia shall follow in the same path.

A. Trollope, *The West Indies and the Spanish Main* (1859), p. 84

Similarly, in 1862, he declared:

A wish that British North America should ever be

severed from England, or that the Australian colonies should ever be so severed, will be by many
Englishmen deemed unpatriotic. But I think that
such severance is to be wished if it be the case that the
colonies standing alone would become more prosperous than they are under British rule. We have
before us an example in the United States of the
prosperity which has attended the rupture of such
old ties [....] And if the States have so risen since
they left their parent's apron string why should not
British North America rise as high?

That the time has as yet come for such a rising I do
not think: but that it will soon come I do most heart-
ily hope.

A. Trollope, *North America* (1862), Vol. 1, p. 29

Throughout the 1860s, 'separatist' ideas and the nature of
the future relationship with the colonies of British settlement were subjects of vigorous discussion. In 1865 a de-
jected Matthew Arnold bewailed Britain's loss of vision and
general decline:

Yes, we arraign her! but she
The weary Titan, with deaf
Ears and labour-dimm'd eyes,
Regarding neither to right
Nor left, goes passively by,
Staggering on to her goal;
Bearing on shoulders immense,
Atlantëan the load,
Wellnigh not to be borne,
Of the too vast orb of her fate.

Matthew Arnold, 'Heine's Grave' (1865), ll. 87–96

However, after the controversy in 1869–70 surrounding the
withdrawal of the last remaining imperial garrisons from
Canada and New Zealand, a public outcry at home and in
the colonies confirmed a more positive assessment of the
imperial relationship. In the 1870s, the idea of an imperial

federation gained popularity as British self-confidence faltered in the face of a deepening trade depression, the loss of British industrial and commercial supremacy in the world, and the growth of rival powers – principally the United States, the recently unified Germany, and an increasingly belligerent Russia. The international scene was thus set not only for a return to neo-mercantilist ideas but for the revival of an expansionist spirit in the 'Age of New Imperialism'.

Early and Mid-Victorian Attitudes Towards Empire

This somewhat gloomy picture, however, does not give an accurate impression of the role of empire, and attitudes towards it, in the early and mid-Victorian years. After 1783 the principle of imperial control was rapidly reasserted in Pitt's India Act (1784), the Canada Act (1791), and the Act of Union with Ireland (1801). No self-governing constitution was granted to any British dependency for 70 years after the surrender at Saratoga.

> Still shall thine empire's fabric stand,
> Admired and feared from land to land,
> Through every circling age renewed,
> Unchanged, unshaken, unsubdued;
> As rocks resist the wildest breeze,
> That sweeps thy tributary seas.
>
> Thomas Peacock, 'The Genius of the Thames'
> (1812), Part 2, XLV, ll. 9–14

The will to rule was not lost:

> [...] as for the colonies, we purpose through Heaven's blessing to retain them a while yet! Shame on us for unworthy sons of brave fathers if we do not. Brave fathers, by valiant blood and sweat, purchased for us, from the bounty of Heaven, rich possessions in all zones; and we, wretched imbeciles, cannot do the function of administering them? And because the accounts do not stand well in the ledger,

our remedy is, not to take shame to ourselves, and repent in sackcloth and ashes, and amend our beggarly imbecilities and insincerities in that as in other departments of our business, but to fling the business overboard, and declare the business itself to be bad. We are a hopeful set of heirs to a big fortune!

Bad state of the ledger will demonstrate that your way of dealing with your colonies is absurd, and urgently in want of reform; but to demonstrate that the Empire itself must be dismembered to bring the ledger straight? O never.

> T. Carlyle, *Latter-Day Pamphlets No. IV: The New Downing Street* (1850), p. 31

It was Great Britain's *duty* to rule:

England will not readily admit that her own children are worth nothing but to be flung out of doors! England looking on her Colonies can say: 'Here are lands and seas, spice-lands, corn-lands, timber-lands, overarched by zodiacs and stars, clasped by many-sounding seas; wide spaces of the Maker's building, fit for the cradle yet of mighty Nations and their sciences and Heroisms. Fertile continents still inhabited by wild beasts are mine, into which all the distressed populations of Europe might pour themselves, and make at once an Old World and a New World human. By the eternal fiat of the gods, this must yet one day be; this, by all the Divine Silences that rule this Universe, silent to fools, eloquent and awful to the hearts of the wise, is incessantly at this moment, and at all moments, commanded to begin to be. Unspeakable deliverance, and new destiny of thousandfold expanded manfulness for all men, dawns out of the Future here. To me has fallen the godlike task of initiating all that: of me and of my Colonies, the abstruse Future asks, Are you wise enough for so sublime a destiny? Are you too foolish?'

> Ibid, pp. 31–2

A new justification for empire, replacing the older props of autocratic government and mercantilism, soon gained popularity: the idea of a great imperial destiny to plant British people and institutions overseas, based on the twin foundations of British emigration to, and investment in, colonies of British settlement. The empire could be used to remedy the social ills of the mother country.

The problem of population growth featured prominently in contemporary thinking after Thomas Malthus, in his *Essay on the Principle of Population* (1798), predicted wholesale starvation in the not too distant future. This preoccupation intensified in the years after the Napoleonic Wars when Great Britain experienced periods of trade depression, chronic unemployment and social unrest. The causes were held to be excess population and a glut of capital: commercial crises, business failures and widespread misery were caused by a fall in profits brought about by too much capital seeking investment. In 1812, Robert Southey wrote:

> We have Canada with all its territory, we have Surinam, the Cape Colony, Australasia [. . .] countries which are more than fifty-fold the area of the British isles, and which a thousand years of uninterrupted prosperity would scarcely suffice to people. It is time that Britain should become the hive of nations, and cast her swarms; and here are lands to receive them. What is required of government is to encourage emigration by founding settlements, and facilitating the means of transportation.

> R. Southey, 'On the State of the Poor, the Principle of Mr. Malthus's Essay on Population, and the Manufacturing System' (1812), in *Essays, Moral and Political* (1832), Vol. 1, p. 154

In such circumstances, Wordsworth felt Great Britain had a 'special cause for joy':

> For, as the element of air affords
> An easy passage to the industrious bees
> Fraught with their burdens; and a way as smooth

> For those ordained to take their sounding flight
> From the thronged hive, and settle where they list
> In fresh abodes – their labour to renew;
> So the wide waters, open to the power,
> The will, the instincts, and appointed needs
> Of Britain, do invite her to cast off
> Her swarms, and in succession send them forth;
> Bound to establish new communities
> On every shore whose aspect favours hope
> Or bold adventure, promising to skill
> And perseverance their deserved reward.

> > William Wordsworth, *The Excursion* (1814), Book 9,
> > ll. 371–82

Samuel Coleridge agreed:

> Colonization is not only a manifest expedient for,
> but an imperative duty on, Great Britain. God seems
> to hold out his finger to us over the sea [. . . .] I think
> this country is now suffering grievously under an
> excessive accumulation of capital, which, having no
> field for profitable operation, is in a state of fierce
> civil war with itself.

> > S. T. Coleridge, 4 May 1833, in T. Ashe (ed.), *The
> > Table Talk and Omniana of Samuel Taylor
> > Coleridge* (1884), p. 216

Carlyle adopted a similar stance in *Sartor Resartus* (1833–4)
and *Chartism* (1839). Edward Gibbon Wakefield finally
brought the various threads of the argument together in a
scheme laid out in *A View of the Art of Colonization* (1849).
    It was John Stuart Mill's conversion, however, which set
the seal of approval on the new doctrines. In his *Principles of
Political Economy* (1848), Mill concluded:

> The exportation of labourers and capital from old to
> new countries, from a place where their productive
> power is less to a place where it is greater, increases
> by so much the aggregate produce of the labour and
> capital of the world. It adds to the joint wealth of the

old and the new country, what amounts in a short period to many times the mere cost of effecting the transport. There needs be no hesitation in affirming that Colonization, in the present state of the world, is the best affair of business, in which the capital of an old and wealthy country can engage.

> J. S. Mill, *Principles of Political Economy* (1848), p. 382

By the 1850s, the settlement colonies were depicted as lands of promise, of prosperity and happiness. In Edward Bulwer-Lytton's *The Caxtons*, Australia becomes a land not of transportation but of redemption. The politician, Trevanion, endorsing 'Sisty' Caxton's decision to emigrate, commends

> sending out not only the paupers, the refuse of an over-populated state, but a large proportion of a better class – fellows full of pith and sap, and exuberant vitality, like yourself, blending [. . .] a certain portion of the aristocratic with the more democratic element; not turning a rabble loose upon a new soil, but planting in the foreign allotments all the rudiments of a harmonious state, analagous to that in the mother country – not only getting rid of hungry craving mouths, but furnishing vent for a waste surplus of intelligence and courage, which at home is really not needed, and more often comes to ill than to good – here only menaces our artificial embankments, but there, carried off in an aqueduct, might give life to a desert.

> E. Bulwer-Lytton, *The Caxtons: A Family Picture* (1849), p. 380

There, Sisty's young companions experience social rehabilitation. Sisty concludes from his experiences:

> There is something in this new soil – in the labour it calls forth, in the hope it inspires, in the sense of property, which I take to be the core of social morals – that expedites the work of redemption with marvellous

rapidity. Take them altogether, whatever their origin, or whatever brought them hither, they are a fine, manly, frank-hearted race, these colonists now!

Ibid, p. 534

In *David Copperfield* (1849–50), New South Wales is the place where the Peggottys prosper and Mr Micawber becomes a colonial magistrate. Dickens also wrote many pro-emigration articles in his weekly periodical, *Household Words*, in the 1850s. When gold was discovered in Australia in 1851, an additional 'get-rich-quick' element was added to the story in Charles Reade's *It is Never Too Late to Mend* (1856), Henry Kingsley's *The Recollections of Geoffrey Hamlyn* (1859), Anthony Trollope's *The Three Clerks* (1858) and *John Caldigate* (1879). In *Australia and New Zealand* (1873), Trollope concluded:

> The life of the artisan there is certainly a better life than he can find at home. He not only lives better, with more comfortable appurtenances around him, but he fills a higher position in reference to those around him, and has a greater consideration paid to him than would have fallen to his lot at home. He gets a better education for his children than he can in England, and may have a more assured hope of seeing them rise above himself, and has less cause to fear that they shall fall infinitely lower. Therefore I would say to any young man whose courage is high and whose intelligence is not below par, that he should not be satisfied to remain at home; but should come out [. . .] and try to win a higher lot and a better fortune than the old country can afford to give him.

A. Trollope, *Australia and New Zealand* (1873), Vol. 1, p. 58

The Mid-Victorian Debate

Clearly, it was not the existence of colonies *per se* that Trollope objected to but their system of management and the humiliating position of dependency after they had reached maturity. The same point was made by most critics of the imperial connection:

> Instead of wishing to separate from our colonies, or to avert the establishment of new ones, I would say distinguish between the evil and the good; remove the evil, but preserve the good; do not 'Emancipate your colonies', but multiply them, and improve – reform your system of colonial government.

W. Molesworth, 6 March 1838, in H. E. Egerton (ed.), *Selected Speeches of Sir William Molesworth on Questions Relating to Colonial Policy* (1903), p. 11

> We hope it is not supposed, from anything now started, that we consider the foundations of colonial establishments as, generally speaking, inexpedient [. . . .] It is not to the establishment of colonies [. . .] but to the trammels that have been laid on their industry, and the interference exercised by the mother country that we object.

J. R. McCulloch, *A Statistical Account of the British Empire* (1837), Vol. 1, p. 593

So far as India was concerned, few advocated separation. Gladstone regarded India as a 'capital demand' upon the nation's honour. Goldwin Smith and John Bright were equally appalled at the thought of its abandonment. Nobody suggested that the empire of trade and strategy – the long chain of naval bases, dockyards, entrepôts and coaling stations across the world – should be got rid of, so vital had it become to British commercial interests. In fact the empire continued to expand at a faster rate than before: in India, British North America, Australia, New Zealand, the Pacific, West and South Africa. In addition, significant bases in world and local trade were acquired at Singapore (1819), Aden (1839), Hong Kong (1842), Labuan (1846) and Kowloon (1860). Thus, while empire may not have had the high profile it enjoyed in the late Victorian years, the early and mid-Victorians were not indifferent to it, as every analysis of parliamentary debates, the press, and contemporary writings indicates. In an age of British dominance, the age of Palmerston and gunboat diplomacy, when Britain was dubbed not only the self-appointed policeman of the world but also its workshop, it was simply not necessary to blow the imperial trumpet so loudly, or so often, or to adopt a policy of belligerent expansionism, when British interests could be secured by more informal political means.

The crux of the mid-Victorian debate was not the extinction of empire. John Roebuck had accurately observed in 1849:

> The people of this country have never acquiesced in the opinion that our colonies are useless; and they look with disfavour on any scheme of policy which contemplates the separation of the mother country from the colonies. For this opinion the people have been seldom able to render an adequate reason; nor have they been accustomed to describe with accuracy the way in which the colonies prove useful to us; still they believe them beneficial, and so believing, they regard with suspicion those who roundly propose 'to cut the connexion'.

J. A. Roebuck, *The Colonies of England* (1849), pp. 8–9

Even Cobden, Bright and Anthony Trollope were in agreement that it was not possible to take a unilateral decision to throw the colonies off.

The subject debated in the mid-Victorian years was the future shape of the empire in terms of government and defence. Lord John Russell, as Prime Minister, admitted:

> I anticipate indeed with others that some of the colonies may so grow in population and wealth that they may say – 'Our strength is sufficient to enable us to be independent of England. The link is now become onerous to us – the time is come when we can, in amity and alliance with England, maintain our independence.' I do not think that that time is yet

approaching. But let us make them as far as possible, fit to govern themselves – let us give them as far as we can, the capacity of ruling their own affairs – let them increase in wealth and population, and whatever may happen, we of this great empire shall have the consolation of saying that we have contributed to the happiness of the world.

Lord John Russell, 8 February 1850, *Hansard*,
Vol. cviii, cols. 566–7

Gladstone, too, looked forward to the 'creation of so many happy Englands':

Govern them upon the principle of freedom – let them not feel any yokes upon their necks – let them understand that the relations between you and them are relations of affection; even in the matter of continuing the connexion, let the colonists be the judges, for they are the best judges as to whether they ought to continue to be with you or not, and rely upon it you will reap a rich reward in the possession of that affection unbroken and unbounded in all the influence which the possession of such colonies will give you, and in all the grandeur it will add to your renown. Defend them from aggression from without – regulate their foreign relations (those things belong to the colonial connexion, but of the duration of that connexion let them be the judges) – and I predict that if you leave them that freedom of judgment it is hard to say when the day will come when they will wish to separate from the great name of England.

'An Address delivered to the Members of the Mechanics' Institute at Chester, 12 November 1855', quoted in P. Knaplund, *Gladstone and Britain's Imperial Policy* (1927), p. 193

And so it proved as the loose ends of responsible

government were tidied up in the 1860s. In fact, the timely devolution of internal administration removed the disadvantages of the connection for both colony and mother country, thus extending the life of that connection into the twentieth century.

Even Goldwin Smith envisaged a continuing relationship:

> That connexion with the Colonies, which is really part of our greatness – the connexion of blood, sympathy and ideas – will not be affected by political separation. And when our Colonies are nations, something in the nature of a great Anglo-Saxon federation may, in substance if not in form, spontaneously arise out of affinity and mutual affection.
>
> G. Smith, *The Empire* (1863), p. 6

It was this feature, the 'virtual confederation of the English race', that was taken up in one of the most influential books of the age: Charles Dilke's *Greater Britain* (1868), a two-volume record of the author's recent journey through the English-speaking world.

Dilke did not believe in empire as an organised system of political relations: his allegiance was to a wider nationalism, to 'Anglo-Saxondom'. Following Goldwin Smith, Dilke was frankly separatist as regards Canada. He could see no reason why Great Britain should be more friendly towards Canada than the United States which offered the English 'race' the 'moral dictatorship of the globe, by ruling mankind through Saxon institutions and the English tongue'. He was more tolerant of the Australasian connection, provided the colonies paid their way. But when it came to the Crown colonies and India, Dilke became positively fervent in favour of their retention:

> The possession of India offers to ourselves that element of vastness of dominion which, in this age, is needed to secure width of vision and nobility of purpose; but to the English our possession of India, of the coast of Africa, and the ports of China offers

the possibility of planting free institutions among the dark-skinned races of the world.

> C. W. Dilke, *Greater Britain* (1868), Vol. 2, p. 40

It was this appeal to the Anglo-Saxon race and English civilization, the emphasis on India and the Crown colonies, the willingness to contemplate expansion (Trollope had opposed expansion in order to better consolidate the existing empire), and the boisterous pride in governing the black and brown-skinned peoples, that set Dilke's book apart. In this respect it provided a neat bridge between the ideas of the mid-and late Victorian ages.

The Empire Fights Back

Dilke's book rapidly went through three editions. Its optimistic vision of an *expansive* future for the Anglo-Saxon race caught public imagination. Its tone, the strong appeal to British pride and the values of the mid-Victorians was in marked contrast to the rest of contemporary writing on the empire, such as the recently published two-volume work by Viscount Bury entitled *The Exodus of the Western Nations* (1865). Most serious writers, accepting the logic of the increasing independence of the settlement colonies, regarded the alternatives as being between planned separation and a policy of 'drift'. Because the British government's colonial policy made no specific arrangements for separation, it was usually stigmatised as being the latter. Hence the abundance of literature in the late 1860s suggesting future paths for the government to take. In contrast, a few writers called for imperial consolidation, an imperial parliament, even for imperial federation. Some began to feel that

> between the alternatives of dependence and separation lies the real secret of a lasting connexion – that of common partnership.

> C. B. Adderley, *Review of 'The Colonial Policy of Lord John Russell's Administration' by Earl Grey, 1853; and of Subsequent Colonial History* (1869), p. 3

In the 1860s, then, the 'colonial question' was well aired. The empire was rarely out of the news. In 1859, a scare concerning a French invasion of Britain led to a defence review, culminating in the 1861 Select Committee on Colonial Military Expenditure which recommended the withdrawal of imperial garrisons. The American Civil War raised the perennial difficulties involved in the defence of Canada. The Maori wars in New Zealand attracted the attention of those who objected to British troops being used for the maintenance of internal security in self-governing colonies. The Ashanti War of 1863–4 nearly brought about the downfall of the Palmerston government and led to the 1865 Select Committee on the West African Settlements. In the West Indies, criticisms of Governor Eyre's heavy-handed quelling of a race riot in Jamaica erupted in a public controversy in which Carlyle, Charles Kingsley, Ruskin, Dickens, Tennyson, John Tyndall, J. S. Mill, Huxley, Darwin, Lyell, Spencer and Thomas Hughes became embroiled, ending in Eyre's much-publicised trial at the Old Bailey. The late 1860s also saw Fenian raids on the new Dominion of Canada, a war against Abyssinia – the first of Queen Victoria's 'little wars' to become a newspaper event – and Riel's rebellion on the Red River. Finally, the decade closed amid heated arguments concerning the withdrawal of the last British regiments from Canada and New Zealand.

Not surprisingly such controversies led the defenders of empire to close ranks. A Colonial Society (the forerunner of the present Royal Commonwealth Society) was founded in 1868, colonial conferences were organised at the Cannon Street Hotel and Westminster Palace Hotel, public meetings were held, renewed calls for state-aided emigration made, and public petitions signed. One petition, signed by 104 000 working men in London, protesting that they had 'heard with alarm that Your Majesty has been advised to give up the colonies', carried the signatures of Carlyle, Tennyson and the historian J. A. Froude. Froude, at his inauguration as Rector at the University of St Andrews, looked forward with enthusiasm to the peopling of new lands:

> Britain may yet have a future before it grander than its past; instead of a country standing alone,

complete in itself, it may become the metropolis of an enormous and coherent Empire.

W. A. Knight (ed.), *Rectorial Addresses delivered at the University of St Andrews, 1863–93* (1894), p. 102

Subsequently in a series of articles written for *Fraser's Magazine*, revealing the influence of Carlyle, Froude denounced the 'cess-pit civilization' of *laisser-faire* and industrialization and stressed that England could remain a great power only by retaining and developing her empire.

Another proselyte and disciple of Carlyle, John Ruskin, the new Professor of Fine Art at Oxford in 1870, also held up colonization as a worthy alternative to Materialism and Mammon-worship:

> There is a destiny now possible to us – the highest ever set before a nation to be accepted or refused [. . .] will you, youths of England, make your country again a royal throne of kings; a sceptred isle, for all the world a source of light, a centre of peace; mistress of Learning and of the Arts; – faithful guardian of great memories in the midst of irreverent and ephemeral visions; – faithful servant of time-tried principles, under temptation from fond experiments and licentious desires; and amidst the cruel and clamorous jealousies of the nations, worshipped in her strange valour, of goodwill towards men? [. . .]
>
> And this is what she must either do, or perish: she must found colonies as fast and as far as she is able, formed of her most energetic and worthiest men; – seizing every piece of fruitful waste ground she can set her foot on, and there teaching these her colonists that their chief virtue is to be fidelity to their country, and that their first aim is to be to advance the power of England by land and by sea; and that, though they live on a distant plot of ground, they are no more to consider themselves therefore disfranchised from their native land, than the sailors of her fleet do, because they float on distant waves [. . .] if we can get men for little pay, to cast themselves

against cannon-mouths for love of England, we may
find men also who will plough and sow for her, who
will behave kindly and righteously for her, who will
bring up their children to love her, and who will
gladden themselves in the brightness of her glory,
more than in all the light of tropic skies [. . . .]
   You think that an impossible ideal. Be it so; refuse
to accept it if you will; but see that you form your
own in its stead. All that I ask of you is to have a
fixed purpose of some kind for your country and
yourselves; no matter how restricted, so that it be
fixed and unselfish.

J. Ruskin, *Lectures on Art* (1905), pp. 41–3

It is frequently claimed that these passages from Ruskin's
Inaugural Lecture later had a dramatic impact on Cecil
Rhodes.
   Two other members of the literary fraternity joined the
fray. One of the lesser brethren, Alfred Austin, attacked
those who did not wish to retain the colonies:

Her very sons, sprung from her mighty loins,
We aliens make, to save some paltry coins;
With our own hands destroy our Empire old,
And stutter, 'All is lost, except our gold!'
With languid limbs, by comfortable fire,
We see our glories, one by one expire;
A Nelson's flag, a Churchill's flashing blade,
Debased to menials of rapacious Trade [. . . .]

A. Austin, 'The Golden Age' (1871), quoted in
N. B. Crowell, *Alfred Austin: Victorian* (1953),
p. 186

Tennyson came to the defence of Canada:

And that true North, whereof we lately heard
A strain to shame us 'keep you to yourselves;
So loyal is too costly! friends – your love
Is but a burthen: loose the bond, and go.'

Is this the tone of empire? here the faith
That made us rulers? this, indeed, her voice
And meaning, whom the roar of Hougoumont
Left mightiest of all peoples under heaven?
What shock has fool'd her since, that she should
        speak
So feebly? wealthier – wealthier – hour by hour!
The voice of Britain, or a sinking land,
Some third-rate isle half-lost among her seas?
There rang her voice, when the full city peal'd
Thee and thy Prince! The loyal to their crown
Are loyal to their own far sons, who love
Our ocean-empire with her boundless homes
For ever-broadening England, and her throne
In our vast Orient, and one isle, one isle,
That knows not her own greatness: if she knows
And dreads it we are fallen.

> Lord Tennyson, 'To the Queen' (1872) added to
> 'Idylls of the King' (1863–9), ll. 14–33

By 1872, continuation of the existing relationship with the colonies of settlement was becoming a popular demand.

To some extent, a new set of circumstances was forging a new outlook on empire. The Franco–Prussian War and the unification of Germany revealed a significant tilt in the balance of power in Europe. The United States was emerging from the throes of civil war and Russia was extending her territory in Asia. The return to protective tariffs also heralded industrial revolutions among Britain's competitors. The Manchester School's vision of a world of peace, of free trade, of a world dominated by the commerce of Great Britain, was fast disappearing. In such circumstances the benefits of empire were reassessed. Even Anthony Trollope revised his earlier opinion in 1873, admitting:

> that some of us in England have been a little too forward in our assurances to the colonies that they have only to speak the word themselves, and they shall be free [. . . .] Separation, though it may be ultimately certain is, I think, too distant to have a place

as yet in the official or parliamentary vocabulary of a
Colonial Minister.

A. Trollope, *Australia and New Zealand* (1873),
Vol. 1, p. 8

The cause of empire prospered in the 1870s. All talk of
policies of 'drift' or separation disappeared as scheme after
scheme for imperial consolidation was put forward. Federation became the talk of the town. The movement reached its
climax in 1884 with the foundation of the Imperial Federation League but collapsed in confusion in 1893 without any
grand design being agreed. The activities of the federation-
ists, therefore, even though Joseph Chamberlain later took
up some of their ideas, provide but a minor theme in the
New Imperialism. Instead, the decade which witnessed the
birth of 'jingoism' saw the birth of a new concept of empire
which focused attention elsewhere, a concept usually associated with the name of one man, the author of *Tancred*,
Benjamin Disraeli.

Disraeli's Contribution to the Imperial Idea

Disraeli, believing that 'ships, colonies and commerce' were
the basis of Britain's greatness, had consistently opposed the
calls of 'prigs and pedants' for the dismemberment of the
empire. He was also critical of the way in which responsible
government had been implemented. In 1872, he seized the
opportunity to promote the empire as one of the three great
concerns of the Conservative party.

On 24 June 1872, in a speech at the Crystal Palace to the
National Union of Conservative and Constitutional Associations, he attempted to reassert his authority as party leader
and to rally the party faithful by highlighting the differences
between the two great political parties. He dubbed the Liberals the 'continental' or 'cosmopolitan' party and the Conservatives the truly 'national' party:

> If you look to the history of this country since the
> advent of Liberalism – forty years ago – you will find
> that there has been no effort so continuous, so subtle,

supported by so much energy, and carried on with so much ability and acumen, as the attempt of Liberalism to effect the disintegration of the Empire of England.

And, gentlemen, of all its efforts, this is the one which has been the nearest to success. Statesmen of the highest character, writers of the most distinguished ability, the most organised and most efficient means, have been employed in this endeavour. It has been proved to all of us that we have lost money by our Colonies. It has been shown with precise, with mathematical demonstration, that there never was a jewel in the Crown of England that was so truly costly as the possession of India. How often has it been suggested that we should at once emancipate ourselves from this incubus! Well, that result was nearly accomplished. When those subtle views were adopted by the country under the plausible plea of granting self-government to the Colonies, I confess that I myself thought that the tie was broken. Not that I for one object to self-government. I cannot conceive how our distant Colonies can have their affairs administered except by self-government.

But self-government, in my opinion, when it was conceded, ought to have been conceded as part of a great policy of Imperial consolidation. It ought to have been accompanied by an Imperial tariff, by securities for the people of England for the enjoyment of the unappropriated lands which belonged to the Sovereign as their trustee, and by a military code which should have precisely defined the means and the responsibilities by which the Colonies should be defended, and by which, if necessary, this country should call for aid from the Colonies themselves. It ought, further, to have been accompanied by the institution of some representative council in the metropolis, which would have brought the Colonies into constant and continuous relations with the Home Government. All this, however, was omitted because those who advised that policy – and I believe their convictions were sincere – looked upon the Colonies of England, looked upon even our connection with India, as a burden upon this country, viewing everything in a financial aspect, and totally passing by those moral and political considerations which make nations great, and by the influence of which alone men are distinguished from animals.

Well, what has been the result of this attempt during the reign of Liberalism for the disintegration of the Empire? It has entirely failed. But how has it failed? Through the sympathy of the Colonies for the Mother Country. They have decided that the Empire shall not be destroyed, and in my opinion no Minister in this country will do his duty who neglects any opportunity of reconstructing as much as possible our Colonial Empire, and of responding to those distant sympathies which may become the source of incalculable strength and happiness to this land [. . . .]

The issue is not a mean one. It is whether you will be content to be a comfortable England, modelled and moulded on Continental principles and meeting in due course an inevitable fate, or whether you will be a great country – an Imperial country – a country where your sons, when they rise, rise to paramount positions, and obtain not merely the esteem of their countrymen, but command the respect of the world.

> T. E. Kebbel (ed.), *Selected Speeches of the Late Earl of Beaconsfield* (1882), Vol. 2, pp. 530–1, 534

This celebrated speech, it has been claimed, began the long connection between Conservatism and empire.

However, Disraeli's speech was not intended as a blueprint for future policy. It was more a criticism in retrospect of earlier Liberal actions. Nor was it a call for expansion. Later events during his 1874–80 ministry – the annexation of the Fiji Islands, the extension of British influence into the interior of the Gold Coast, the establishment of the resident system in several Malay States, and the annexation of the Transvaal – gave Disraeli the reputation for being an expansionist. But Disraeli took no interest in these events. Even the Zulu War was the result of his inexperienced Colonial Secretary's failure to control a determined colonial governor. Only in the case of the second Afghan War can Disraeli be said to have played a part. But even here, despite Disraeli's public bluster about a 'scientific frontier', he was privately furious at the Viceroy's action in bringing on war. Disraeli was not interested in colonial affairs but in the part the empire could play in adding to Britain's power and prestige in the world.

It is not surprising, then, that it was Disraeli's conduct of Indian affairs and foreign policy – his dramatic personal coup in acquiring 44 per cent of the Suez Canal Company shares, the creation of the Queen as Empress of India and, above all, his brinkmanship during the Eastern Question crisis rushing Indian troops to Malta and occupying Cyprus without consulting parliament – that led to so much controversy.

Edward Dicey, the editor of *The Observer*, became the spokesman for an illiberal and undemocratic imperial spirit. The British empire, he claimed, was established for the sole benefit of Great Britain:

> We too have followed our star, fulfilled our destiny, worked out the will implanted in us; and to say that we have been influenced in the main by any higher motive seems to me self-deception. Still though to assert that we have gone forth to foreign lands for the sake of doing good would be sheer hypocrisy, we may fairly say that we have done good by going and are doing good by stopping [. . . .]

> E. Dicey, 'Mr. Gladstone and Our Empire', *The Nineteenth Century* (September, 1877), Vol. 2, p. 300

Disraeli's rhetoric heightened the controversy:

> I have ever considered that Her Majesty's Government, of whatever party formed, are the trustees of that Empire. That Empire was formed by the energy and enterprise of your ancestors, my lords; and it is

one of a very peculiar character. I know no example of it, either in ancient or modern history. No Caesar or Charlemagne ever presided over a dominion so peculiar. Its flag floats on many waters; it has provinces in every zone, they are inhabited by persons of different races, different religion, different laws, manners, customs. Some of these are bound to us by ties of liberty, fully conscious that without their connection with the metropolis they have no security for public freedom and self-government; others are bound to us by flesh and blood and by material as well as moral considerations. There are millions who are bound to us by our military sway, and they bow to that sway because they know that they are indebted to it for order and justice. All these communities agree in recognising the commanding spirit of these islands that has formed and fashioned in such a manner so great a proportion of the globe.

> Earl of Beaconsfield, House of Lords, 8 April 1878,
> T. E. Kebbel (ed.), *Selected Speeches of the Late
> Earl of Beaconsfield*, Vol. 2, p. 177

On his return from the Congress of Berlin, Disraeli flaunted the military concept of empire:

Her Majesty has fleets and armies that are second to none. England must have seen with pride the Mediterranean covered with her ships; she must have seen with pride the discipline and devotion which have been shown to her and her Government by all her troops, drawn from every part of her Empire. I leave it to the illustrious duke [the Duke of Cambridge] in whose presence I speak, to bear witness to the spirit of imperial patriotism which has been exhibited by the troops from India, which he recently reviewed at Malta. But it is not on our fleets and armies, however necessary they may be for the maintenance of imperial strength, that I alone or mainly depend in that enterprise on which this country is about to enter. It is on what I most highly value – the consciousness that in the

Eastern Nations there is a confidence in this country,
and that, while we know that we can enforce our
policy, at the same time they know that our Empire
is an Empire of liberty, of truth, and of justice.

Earl of Beaconsfield, House of Lords, 18 July 1878,
Hansard, Vol. ccxli, cols. 1753–4

It was in this atmosphere that Tennyson penned 'The
Revenge' (1878) and 'The Defence of Lucknow' (1879), that
'jingoism' first saw the light of day, and Disraeli's aggressive
and apparently expansionist foreign and imperial policies
came to be dubbed 'Beaconsfieldism'.

A new imperial age was being born. In the eyes of his
critics, the empire was becoming a centralised military unit,
beyond the control of parliament, which, at the behest of the
British Prime Minister, was being used to further purely
British ends. Gladstone thundered:

> Territorial aggrandisement, backed by military dis-
> play, is the *chevaille de bataille* of the administra-
> tion. Empire is greatness; leagues of land are empire;
> your safety is measured by the fear you strike into
> other nations; trade follows the flag; he that doubts is
> an enemy to his country [. . . .] The Government, not
> uniformly nor consistently, but in the main and on
> the whole, have opened up and relied on an illegitim-
> ate source of power, which never wholly fails: they
> have appealed under the prostituted name of patriot-
> ism, to exaggerated fears, to imaginary interests, and
> to the acquisitiveness of a race which has surpassed
> every other known to history in the faculty of appro-
> priating to itself vast spaces of the earth, and estab-
> lishing its supremacy over men of every race and
> language [. . . .]
>   Between the two parties in this controversy there is a
> perfect agreement that England has a mighty mission in
> the world; but there is a discord as fundamental upon
> the question what that mission is [. . . .] It is the
> administrative connexion, and the shadow of political

subordination, which chiefly give them value in the sight of the party, who at home as well as abroad are striving to cajole us into Imperialism. With their opponents it is the welfare of these communities which forms the great object of interest and desire.

W. E. Gladstone, 'England's Mission', *The Nineteenth Century* (September, 1878), Vol. 4, pp. 368–72

The Liberal view of empire was one of growing communities, freely associated, bound to the mother country by ties of kindred and affection, of friendship and trust.

Thus began an ideological battle over the two views of empire which dominated political debate for the next 50 years. In 1879, a satirical biography of Disraeli in verse declared:

> Imperialism will never do
> Where Hampden, Cromwell, had a birth;
> Our fathers' spirit doth imbue
> Their children all the wide world through,
> And now they know its worth!
> Imperialism! what is it, save
> Presumptuous arrogance and pride? –
> A monstrous self love that would crave
> All for its own of good and brave –
> Self-crowned, self-deified!
> A huge monstrosity of lies,
> And juggling and double dealing,
> And lofty-handed tyrannies,
> And barbarous, brutal cruelties,
> Inhuman and unfeeling.

J. G. Ashworth, *Imperial Ben. A Jew d'Esprit* (1879), p. 75

A policy of 'occupy, fortify, grab and brag' was how Lord Derby (who defected to the Liberals in 1880) described his former leader's actions.

Gladstone kept up the momentum of his attack on

'Beaconsfieldism' during two whirlwind tours of Midlothian in 1879 and 1880. The fickle British public, who had cheered Disraeli on his return from the Congress of Berlin, now warmed to Gladstone's denunciations of imperialist ventures, reckless expenditure, and unpopular wars. By the General Election of 1880, 'imperialism' had become a damaging political smear-word and Disraeli's manifesto was ignominiously rejected at the polls.

But Disraeli's imperial spirit glorifying British achievements and rule overseas lived on. Patriotism and empire had begun to be linked in a way undreamed of in Palmerston's day. Even Tennyson's verse was becoming more jingoistic. In a revised version of 'Hands all Round' he wrote:

> To all the loyal hearts who long
>   To keep our English Empire whole!
> To all our noble sons, the strong
>   New England of the Southern Pole!
> To England under Indian skies,
>   To those dark millions of her realm!
> To Canada whom we love and prize
>   Whatever statesman holds the helm!
>   Hands all round!
>   God the traitor's hope confound!
> To this great name of England drink, my friends,
>   And all her glorious empire, round and round.

Lord Tennyson, 'Hands All Round' (1882), ll. 13–24

Appropriately, the following year witnessed the publication of one of the best-selling books about empire, a book which perhaps did more than any other to establish the aura of confidence in empire so evident in the late nineteenth century.

Academic Respectability

Sir John Seeley's eloquent lectures to his Cambridge students in 1881–2 were published in 1883 under the title *The Expansion of England*. His purpose was to heighten the historical consciousness of his students. He began:

It is a favourite maxim of mine that history, while it should be scientific in its method, should pursue a practical object. That is, it should not merely gratify the reader's curiosity about the past, but modify his view of the present and his forecast of the future. Now if this maxim be sound, the history of England ought to end with something that might be called a moral. Some large conclusion ought to arise out of it; it ought to exhibit the general tendency of English affairs in such a way as to set us thinking about the future and divining the destiny which is reserved for us.

J. R. Seeley, *The Expansion of England* (1883), p. 1

Seeley identified the 'tendency' of the last two centuries, the clue which bound together the past and future of England, as the creation of 'Greater Britain', the expansion of the English state in the New World and in India. What was the moral? At present, Seeley wrote,

There are two schools of opinion among us with respect to our Empire, of which schools the one may be called the bombastic and the other the pessimistic. The one is lost in wonder and ecstacy at its immense dimensions, and at the energy and heroism which presumably have gone to the making of it; this school therefore advocates the maintenance of it as a point of honour or sentiment. The other is in the opposite extreme, regards it as founded in aggression and rapacity, as useless and burdensome, a kind of excrescence upon England, as depriving us of the advantages of our insularity and exposing us to wars and quarrels in every part of the globe; this school therefore advocates a policy which may lead at the earliest possible opportunity to the abandonment of it.

Ibid, pp. 293–4

Seeley would have truck with neither school. There was

nothing glorious in the possession of vast territory, unless the component parts existed for mutual benefit, and to regard colonies as the property of the mother country simply repeated the mistakes which had led to the loss of the American colonies. On the other hand, to ask the question what was the good of colonies showed that the speaker did not regard the self-governing colonists as Englishmen overseas and the colonies as integral parts of England. Nobody asked whether Cornwall or Kent paid their way. The English should cease thinking of themselves as an island off the north-western coast of Europe and instead view themselves as part of a great homogeneous people, in blood, language, religion and laws dispersed over a boundless space. Science was removing the problems of distance and federal structures made vast political unions possible. If the United States and Russia held together, they would dwarf the old powers of Europe in 50 years' time. If the British empire constituted one nationality, Great Britain would remain great as the third superpower.

Seeley's justification for the retention of empire was as logical as Goldwin Smith's statement of the case for dismemberment in 1863. Moreover, his bold assertions that empire had nothing to do with calculations of profit and loss, and that the eventual independence of colonies of British settlement was not a law of nature but dependent on their management, challenged the central tenets of earlier 'separatist' writings. No matter that Seeley ignored the growth of separate colonial nationalities and the position of India and the Crown colonies: few contemporaries concerned themselves with such problems. It did not matter that Seeley's ideas were unoriginal. Seeley's *The Expansion of England* succeeded admirably in providing its readers with an optimistic view, a convincing imperial vision of the future. That Seeley also succeeded in increasing the awareness of empire among a much wider audience than his students is shown by the volume's sales: 80 000 copies in the first two years. It remained continuously in print until 1956, a new paperback edition appearing in 1971.

It is noticeable, however, that Seeley, did not advocate imperial expansion. He showed little interest in the areas outside the settlement colonies, India and the West Indies.

Even his 'bombastic school' was not a reference to jingoism but to Disraeli's romantic concept of empire. Clearly, while the scene was set in the early 1880s for the New Imperialism, not all the actors were yet in place. There was still no mass wave of public interest in imperial expansion nor much concern about the tropics. Developments in the 1880s, however, changed all that and began the education of the schoolboy masters of the world.

2 The Imperial Adventure

There has, indeed, arisen a taste for exotic literature: people have become alive to the strangeness and fascination of the world beyond the bounds of Europe and the United States. But that is only because men of imagination and literary skill have been the new conquerors, the Corteses and Balboas of India, Africa, Australia, Japan and the isles of the southern seas. All such writers [...] have gone out of the streets of the over-populated lands into the open air; have sailed and ridden, walked and hunted; have escaped from the smoke and fog of towns. New strength has come from fresher air into their brains and blood; hence the novelty and buoyancy of the stories which they tell. Hence, too, they are rather to be counted among the romanticists than realists, however real is the essential truth of their books.

Andrew Lang, *Essays in Little* (1891), p. 198

The 1880s witnessed the flowering of a new genre: for adults the imperial romances of Rider Haggard and for children the imperial adventure stories of G. A. Henty, Dr Gordon Stables and a host of others.

The reasons for the emergence of this new genre are complex. In part, the increasing fascination with the world beyond Europe was a natural product of contemporary events. The slave trade, missionary and humanitarian endeavours, the exploration of Africa, the evolution of new racial theories, and the 'little wars' of Victoria's reign, created a great deal of interest in the exotic places of the world, thus providing moral, religious and scientific reasons for taking an interest in black, brown, yellow and red-skinned peoples. In addition, following the education reforms of 1870, the creation of free Board Schools led to an increased demand for juvenile and popular literature. Technological developments also facilitated, for the first time, the production of cheap books and newspapers. Finally, the launch of the new style of adventure story was to some extent a deliberate ploy designed to counteract the popularity of the notorious 'penny dreadfuls' (mainly stories of glamourised violence and crime which were thought to undermine society's values).

Concern about the material popular with the young prompted the creation of numerous children's magazines of an approved type. The more overtly pious character of mid-nineteenth-century children's fiction:

> My heart sank within me; but at that moment my thoughts turned to my beloved mother, and I remembered those words, which were among the last that she said to me – 'Ralph, my dearest child, always remember in the hour of danger to look to your Lord and Saviour Jesus Christ. He alone is both able and willing to save your body and your soul.' So I felt much comforted when I thought thereon.
>
> R. M. Ballantyne, *The Coral Island* (1857), p. 8

was quietly shelved. Instead, from the historical romances of Charles Kingsley, the sea-faring stories of Captain Marryat, the evangelical novels of W. H. G. Kingston and the 'Robin-sonades' of R. M. Ballantyne developed one of the greatest children's adventure stories of all time, complete with its own boy hero and narrator: Robert Louis Stevenson's *Treasure Island* (1883). In turn, the elements of this story were translated to an African setting and merged with the popular romance of Sir Walter Scott, the action being moved from the medieval chivalric past to the exotic and savage present. Rider Haggard's *King Solomon's Mines* (1885) was an immediate best-seller. About the same time, G. A. Henty published three boys' books on the beginnings of empire in India and the recent Ashanti, Zulu and Boer Wars: *With Clive in India* (1884), *By Sheer Pluck* (1884) and *The Young Colonists* (1885). By the mid-1880s the imperial adventure story was firmly established as a popular form of light reading. Its influence and impact was tremendous, lasting well beyond the age of the New Imperialism.

The education of the schoolboy masters of the world had begun. A host of writers essayed to quench the thirst of the newly literate juvenile reader. What better setting for stirring adventure stories and displays of valour than the empire? And what better source for the young hero than the British public schoolboy:

> a typical public schoolboy, straight and clean-limbed, free from all awkwardness, bright in expression, and possessed of a fair amount of 'cheek', a little particular about the set of his Eton jacket, and the appearance of his boots; as hard as nails and almost tireless – the class by which Britain has been built up, her colonies formed, and her battle fields won – a class in point of energy, fearlessness, the spirit of adventure and a readiness to face and overcome all difficulties, unmatched in the world.

> G. A. Henty, *With Roberts to Pretoria* (1902), p. 6

– the type made familiar by Thomas Hughes' *Tom Brown's Schooldays* (1857).

These stories of derring-do, of British heroism and triumphs in distant parts of the world, provided the 'energising myth' of the late Victorian empire. The stories the nation told its children as they went to sleep, helped to colour future responses and shape future values. And, as the young readers outgrew W. H. G. Kingston, Captain Mayne Reid, G. A. Henty, Gordon Stables and F. S. Brereton, they could turn to Rider Haggard, Rudyard Kipling, Joseph Conrad, and to John Buchan (*Prester John*), A. E. W. Mason (*The Four Feathers*) and Edgar Wallace (*Sanders of the River*).

The reading public had very little idea where literary art finished and life began. Most writers endorsed images that were already well formed. Thus, when younger generations went abroad, they took with them preconceived ideas about the world gained mainly from children's fiction, school textbooks, Sunday school tracts and the popular press. Not surprisingly, in the main, they found what they expected.

One colonial administrator in Ceylon (now Sri Lanka) later marvelled:

> The white people were also in many ways astonishingly like characters in a Kipling story. I could never make up my mind whether Kipling had moulded his characters accurately in the image of Anglo-Indian society, or whether we were moulding our characters accurately in the image of a Kipling story.
>
> Leonard Woolf, *Growing: An Autobiography of the Years 1904–1911* (1961), p. 46

Most of these writers helped to create a stereotyped picture of the British and of the rest of the world, a British world-view, which is by no means entirely extinct today. This demonstrates only too clearly the role of such novels, with their patriotism, militarism, racial pride and value judgements, in reflecting, legitimising and romanticising key aspects of the New Imperialism in the late nineteenth century.

From the Penny Dreadful to a Halfpenny Harmsworth

Concern about the material available to the literate classes was not new to the 1880s. From the late eighteenth century attempts had been made to direct reading habits. The foundation of the Sunday school movement had been accompanied by the establishment of religious publishing societies, such as the Religious Tract Society (RTS), to provide material of a suitably improving nature. However, while the output of magazines, tracts and stories was commendable, their pious and highly moral content, as well as the obvious instructional purpose, limited their appeal. Hence the popularity in the 1830s of the 'penny dreadfuls' with their Gothic horror stories and tales of crime and violence in which authority was held up to ridicule and wrong-doers often escaped punishment. Their corrupting influence on society was as much discussed in the mid-nineteenth century as that of 'video nasties' today.

By the 1850s the evangelical publishing houses recognised the need to alter their approach if they were to win back readers, a need made more urgent by the spread of the penny bloods to the juvenile market with such weekly titles as *The Bad Boys' Paper* and *The Wild Boys of London*. Fortunately, the abolition of the repressive newspaper stamp tax in 1861, the development of rotary presses and mechanical typesetting devices, the adoption of new bookbinding techniques and cardboard covers, and the introduction of inexpensive pulp paper, made possible the mass production and mass circulation of cheap popular editions of the classics, missionary writings, travel and exploration stories, lives of great men, and accounts of naval and military engagements – suitable tales of adventure and excitement to satisfy the thirst of the new reading public.

Thus an attempt was made to combat the influence of the penny dreadfuls not only by presenting morality in a more secular and interesting way but by diverting the appeal of violence and aggression into more acceptable channels. R. M. Ballantyne, author of *The Coral Island* (1857), included scenes of violence and bloody descriptions of the chase in his stories, a style readily adopted by Rider Haggard many of whose books, popular as school and Sunday school prizes, oozed blood on every page. Even the evangelical writer, W. H. G. Kingston, was sometimes tempted to play up the military aspects of his stories.

It was the RTS, however, which scored the most spectacular success in 1879 with its launch of the *Boy's Own Paper*, a popular penny weekly which remained in circulation until 1967. Among the more noteworthy of its companions were the short-lived *Union Jack* (1880–3), edited by Kingston and then Henty, with R. L. Stevenson, Conan Doyle and Jules Verne as contributors, *Chums* (1892–1934), and *The Captain* (1899–1924). For working-class lads there were *The Halfpenny Marvel* (1893–1922), *Union Jack* (1894–1933), *Pluck* (1894–1916) ('A High Class Weekly Library of Adventure at Home & Abroad On Land and Sea') and *The Boys' Friend* (1895–1927). A typical advert ran:

Herewith is given one of the many illustrations from the powerful story which will appear in the 'Halfpenny Marvel', on sale next Wednesday. The author is Mr. Herbert Maxwell, who has already found a place in the hearts of all true lovers of stirring and healthy fiction. 'To the Sultan's Rescue' deals with the horrors, treachery and mystery surrounding the notorious Sepaul Rebellion in India and is full of excitement from start to finish. 'To the Sultan's Rescue' is but another instance of how Englishmen, notwithstanding the thousand lurking dangers with which they are surrounded, still preserve an upright and fearless demeanour, and do not shrink from facing odds for the honour of their Queen and for the glory of their country, which calls forth from their country unqualified praise and sincere reverence. The 'Halfpenny Marvel' will be on sale at all newsagents on Wednesday next.

The Union Jack, 22 September 1895, Vol. 3, No. 70

By the late 1890s such journals had become the mouthpiece among working-class adolescents not simply of patriotism but of jingoism. In many eyes, Alfred Harmsworth's answer to the penny dreadful turned out to be a halfpenny dreadfuller.

In the process, however, the violence and the rebellion in the penny dreadfuls had been successfully diverted overseas and utilised in the service of empire. The use of force was seen as an acceptable adjunct to the spread of civilization and Christianity. Social Darwinian precepts condoned the elimination of the most 'inferior' races and legitimised the use of force in the subordination of the rest. This blend of nationalism, militarism and racism was perfectly acceptable to parents, teachers, the Church, the Establishment and the military, especially as it attracted a mass following across the classes creating a unified outlook, competition being with other races and other nationalities. The qualities celebrated were those of valour, physical endurance, loyalty and patriotic self-sacrifice.

The literature was riddled with middle-class values. The

boy heroes who provided models for their peers often attended a public school, played middle-class games (cricket and rugby) and entered middle-class professions. The emphasis was on the development of 'character' and the creation of a ruling race, thus reinforcing the late-Victorian world-view. These were the ideas and values the youth of Britain were exposed to, as they read their comics, books and magazines. In this way the foundations of imperial ideology, to which so many later subscribed, were laid.

It was no coincidence that the writers of popular adventure fiction (as opposed to the literature of feelings embodied in the domestic novel) were men of action. R. M. Ballantyne worked for the Hudson's Bay Company. G. A. Henty was a well-known war correspondent. Gordon Stables had been a naval surgeon. R. L. Stevenson ended his days in Samoa. Rider Haggard helped run up the British flag at Pretoria when the Transvaal was annexed. Joseph Conrad travelled the world as a master mariner. Conan Doyle went out to South Africa as a physician during the Boer War. Edgar Wallace worked as a journalist for the *Daily Mail* and was also Reuter's South African correspondent. John Buchan, one of Milner's kindergarten, later became Governor-General of Canada. While all these men loved England, they also found the confines of its shores stifling. They would have sympathised with Sir Henry Curtis:

> I'm tired [. . .] of doing nothing but play the squire in a country that is sick of squires. For a year or more I have been getting as restless as an old elephant who scents danger. I am always dreaming of Kukuanaland and Gagool and King Solomon's Mines. I can assure you that I have become the victim of an almost unaccountable craving. I am weary of shooting pheasants and partridges, and want to have a go at some large game again. There, you know the feeling – when once one has tasted brandy and water, milk becomes insipid to the palate.

H. Rider Haggard, *Allan Quatermain* (1887), p. 16

Somerset Maugham's Alec Mackenzie had similar feelings:

> 'Already I can hardly bear my impatience when I think of the boundless country and the enchanting freedom', he told a friend. 'Here one grows so small, so mean; but in Africa everything is built to a noble standard. There the man is really a man. There one knows what are will and strength and courage.'
>
> W. S. Maugham, *The Explorer* (1907), pp. 276–7

It was no accident that these writers frequently chose Africa, a continent most of them had visited, as a setting for their stories.

The African Setting

> True, by this time it was not a blank space any more. It had got filled since my boyhood with rivers and lakes and names. It had ceased to be a blank space of delightful mystery – a white patch for a boy to dream gloriously over. It had become a place of darkness.
>
> J. Conrad, *Heart of Darkness* (1902), p. 6

As Africa was charted during the nineteenth century, the dramatic image of 'darkest Africa' took hold. By mid-century it was firmly fixed.

In the early part of the century attention focused on the slave trade and its abolition. It was the subject of numerous poems by Wordsworth, Coleridge, Southey, Byron and Shelley. Perhaps the most famous lines are by Blake:

> My mother bore me in the southern wild
> And I am black, but O my soul is white!
> White as an angel is the English child,
> But I am black, as if bereav'd of light.
>
> William Blake, 'The Little Black Boy' (1789), ll. 1–4

In 1823 William Wilberforce, the champion of abolition, claimed:

> That such a system should so long have been suffered to exist in any part of the British Empire will appear, to our posterity, almost incredible. It had, indeed, been less surprising, if its seat had been in regions, like those of Hindostan, for instance, where a vast population had come into our hands in all the full-blown enormity of heathen institutions; where the bloody superstitions and the unnatural cruelties and immoralities of paganism, had established themselves in entire authority, and had produced their natural effects in the depravity and moral degradation of the species; though even in such a case as that, our excuse would hold good no longer than for the period which might be necessary for reforming the native abuses by those mild and reasonable means which alone are acknowledged to be just in principle, or practically effectual to their purpose. But in communities formed from their very origin by a Christian people, and in colonies containing no Pagan inhabitants but those whom we have ourselves compulsorily brought into it, – inhabitants, too, who, from all the circumstances of their case, had the strongest possible claims on us, both for the reparation of their wrongs, and the relief of their miseries, – such a system should have been continued for two centuries, and by people who may, nevertheless, I trust, be affirmed to be the most moral and humane of nations, is one of those anomalies which, if it does not stagger the belief, will, at least, excite the astonishment of future ages.
>
> W. Wilberforce, *An Appeal to the Religion, Justice, and Humanity of the Inhabitants of the British Empire, In Behalf of the Negro Slaves in the West Indies* (1823), pp. 32–3

Tennyson rejoiced at the abolition of slavery in the West

Indies at the cost of £20 000 000 compensation to the former slave owners:

> O mother Britain lift thou up,
>   Lift up a joyful brow,
> There lies not in the circled seas
>   A land so great as thou.
>
> O let the far-off shores be glad,
>   The isles break out in song,
> For thou didst buy them with a price
>   To ransom them from wrong.
>
> A time may come: this world of men
>   Shall roll in broader light,
> But never shall this world forget
>   Who taught the peoples right.
>
> O let the hills of canes rejoice,
>   The palmy valleys ring!
> What other people old or young
>   Had done so just a thing?

> Lord Tennyson, 'O mother Britain lift thou up'
> (1833–4), ll. 1–16

But the abolition of slavery in British territories only provided another challenge: the stamping out of slavery in other parts of the world and the introduction of Christianity and 'legitimate' commerce in its place. Fowell Buxton, Wilberforce's successor, declared:

> A nobler achievement now invites us. I believe that Great Britain can, if she will, under the favour of the Almighty, confer a blessing on the human race. It may be that at her bidding a thousand nations now steeped in wretchedness, in brutal ignorance, in devouring superstition, possessing but the one trade, and that one the foulest evil that ever blighted prosperity, or poisoned domestic peace, shall, under British tuition, emerge from their debasement, enjoy a long line of blessings – education, agriculture, commerce, peace,

industry and wealth that springs from it; and, far above all, shall willingly receive that religion which, while it confers innumerable temporal blessings, opens the way to an eternal futurity of happiness.

Sir Thomas Fowell Buxton,
The African Slave Trade and its Remedy
(2nd edn, 1840), pp. 528–9

Unfortunately, the abolitionists' constant portrayal of Africa as a land of superstition and cruelty, of savagery and human sacrifice, put an end to eighteenth-century ideas of the 'noble savage'. The missionaries also inadvertently added to the image of 'darkest Africa' by emphasising in their writings and propaganda both the perilousness of their position and the evil customs of the degenerate Africans. The disastrous failure of Buxton's 1841 Niger expedition was a further setback for their cause. Dickens in *Bleak House* poked fun at and indicated the futility of Mrs Jellyby's philanthropic intentions by setting the Borrioboola-Gha mission on the Niger. In his view, attempts at civilizing 'ignorant and savage races' were a waste of time. Like Carlyle, he believed that both humanitarian and missionary would be better employed attending to the poverty and problems of 'darkest England'.

It was, however, the explorers and, above all, that greatest of missionary explorers, David Livingstone, who caught the British public's imagination. The publication of his *Missionary Travels* in 1857, which sold 70 000 copies in three months, made Livingstone into a national hero. He urged an attentive audience:

I beg to direct your attention to Africa. I know that in a few years I shall be cut off in that country, which is now open; do not let it be shut again! I go back to Africa to try to make an open path for commerce and Christianity; do you carry out the work which I have begun. I LEAVE IT WITH YOU!

W. Monk (ed.), *Dr. Livingstone's Cambridge Lectures*
(1858), p. 24

His audience needed little encouragement. The search for the source of the White Nile, the explorations of Richard Burton, J. H. Speke, J. A. Grant, Samuel Baker, Verney Lovett Cameron, Joseph Thomson and Henry Morton Stanley, raised British temperatures. Perhaps no passage was more avidly read than Stanley's description of how he found Livingstone:

> I pushed back the crowds, and passing from the rear walked down a living avenue of people, till I came in front of the semi-circles of Arabs, in front of which stood a whiteman [. . . .] As I advanced slowly towards him I noticed he was pale, looked weary, had a grey beard, wore a bluish cap with a faded gold band around it, and had on a red sleeved waistcoat and a pair of grey tweed trousers. I would have run to him, only I was a coward in the presence of such a mob – would have embraced him, only, he being an Englishman, I did not know how he would receive me; so I did what cowardice and false pride suggested was the best thing – walked deliberately to him; took off my hat and said: [. . . .]

> H. M. Stanley, *How I Found Livingstone* (1872), pp. 411–12

The greeting does not need to be repeated, the immortal words are remembered today.

Stanley published two other best-sellers: *Through the Dark Continent* (1878) and *In Darkest Africa* (1890). In fact, most of the explorers wrote accounts of their expeditions. They were real life adventure tales in which intrepid explorers overcame human and geographical obstacles on triumphant journeys across a dark continent. Indeed, not content with writing non-fiction and undertaking lecture tours, many also wrote fictional romances: S. R. Baker, *Up by the Sea* (1860); J. Thomson and E. Harris Smith, *Ulu: An African Romance* (1888); H. M. Stanley, *My Kalulu: Prince, King and Slave* (1889); and V. L. Cameron, *The Adventures* of *Herbert Massey in Eastern Africa* (1888) and *In Savage Africa: or the Adventures of Frank Baldwin from the Gold Coast to Zanzibar* (1911).

But the British public's thirst for stirring tales of adventure in exotic parts of the world was not fed by exploration alone. Military adventure was another important ingredient. Once again Africa figured prominently: the wars against Abyssinia, Asante, the Zulus, the Boers, the Mahdi, the Ndebele, and so the list goes on. All these events were followed avidly in the newspapers. Once again, the accounts of participants were read with mounting excitement: Father Ohrwalder's *Ten Years Captivity in the Mahdi's Camp* (1892); Slatin Pasha's *Fire and Sword in the Sudan* (1896); R. S. S. Baden-Powell's *The Matabele War* (1897); G. W. Steevens' *With Kitchener to Khartum* (1898); Winston Churchill's *The River War* (1899). Exactly the same is true of India.

Few doubted that the British were born to conquer and to rule. No wonder Cecil Rhodes, in the first draft of his will in 1875, provided for the creation of a secret society to promote:

> the extension of British rule throughout the world [. . .] the colonization by British subjects of all the lands where the means of livelihood are attainable by energy, labour, and enterprise, and especially the occupation by British settlers of the entire continent of Africa, the Holy Land, the Valley of the Euphrates, the islands of Cyprus and Candia, the whole of South America, the islands of the Pacific not heretofore possessed by Great Britain, the whole of the Malay Archipelago, the sea-board of China and Japan, the ultimate recovery of the United States of America as an integral part of the British empire [. . . .]

> Lewis Michell, *The Life of the Rt. Hon. Cecil Rhodes* (1910), Vol. 1, p. 68

Clearly, the imperial adventure genre was ideally suited to the age.

Henty's Chapter of Adventures

Henty was equally a man of his times. The burly hero of schoolboy readers had led an extremely active life. After service in the Crimea when he also acted briefly as a special correspondent for the *Morning Advertiser*, he obtained a full-time appointment on *The Standard*. During the next ten years he travelled the world. He went with Lord Napier's expedition to Abyssinia in 1867–8 (publishing his despatches as *The March to Magdala*), witnessed the opening of the Suez Canal in 1869, covered the Franco–Prussian War and was in Paris during the period of the Commune. Subsequently, he reported the Russo–Turcoman War of 1873, went with Wolseley to Ashanti in 1873–4 (writing up his experiences in *The March to Coomassie*), covered the Carlist insurrection in Spain in 1874, accompanied the Prince of Wales on a lengthy tour of India in 1875, and finally ended his career as a war correspondent in the Turco–Serbian War of 1876. Following a breakdown in his health, he devoted the rest of his life to writing. An unsuccessful author of 12 adult novels, he found his true métier in writing for boys over 80 adventure stories whose eventual sales may have topped 25 000 000.

Henty's impact on the youth of his day (and, at the very least, on two subsequent generations), can be judged from a rather exaggerated attack in the pages of *The Captain* for 1908:

> There is no doubt that the immortal Henty and his hosts of imitators have made the British nation the most conceited people on this earth. It is the plotless trash of authors who shelter themselves behind the section in the library catalogue entitled 'Books for Boys', which has given the average young Englishman that very excellent opinion of himself which he now enjoys. Putting aside the question of the utter impossibilities of the usual boys' book, it is quite easy to see the harm the authors of these volumes cause by the exaggeration of the deeds and opinions of their *invraisemblables* heroes. After fourteen or fifteen years perusal of 'piffle' written apparently for

> his education, the young Englishman leaves home
> and country with the very firm idea in his head that
> he, personally, is equal to two or more Frenchmen,
> about four Germans, an indefinite number of Rus-
> sians, and any quantity you care to mention of the
> remaining scum of the earth.
>
> R. van Eeghen, *The Captain*, May 1908, xix, p. 155

The letter caused a storm of protest.

It is true, however, that Henty's stories had mechanical
plots and stereotyped heroes. The hero was usually a 15- or
16-year-old boy of upper-middle-class origin, sometimes a
public school boy, who through some misfortune has
fallen on hard times and goes abroad to seek fame and fortune. He usually becomes involved in a number of thrilling
escapades, meets famous people and participates in momen-
tous events. Eventually, fame acquired, honour restored and
family fortunes replenished, he returns home, perhaps to
marry, normally settling down to the comfortable life of a
prosperous landowner. The settings range from pre-
Christian times to the beginning of the twentieth century.
Henty soon found that contemporary or near contemporary
settings were the most popular. He devoted about a third of
his stories to imperial themes with such titles as: *With Buller
in Natal*, *At the Point of a Bayonet*, *With Roberts to Pretoria*,
To Herat and Cabul, *With Kitchener in the Soudan*, *With the
Allies to Pekin*, and *Through Three Campaigns*. The fast-
moving events and somewhat stilted dialogue are usually
interlaced with factual descriptions, solid chunks of historical narrative rather clumsily inserted (frequently by an am-
anuensis). Henty's intention was to teach his readers some
history and inculcate the correct manly values, the moral
code of the English gentleman. His fiction helped to spread the
public school code of behaviour to a non-élitist readership.

Henty's heroes embodied Victorian middle-class virtues but
lacked personality and individuality. They conformed to an
accepted mould. Charlie Marryat is a classic example: he was

> slight in build, but his schoolfellows knew that Char-
> lie Marryat's muscles were as firm and hard as those

of any boy in the school. In all sports requiring activity and endurance rather than weight and strength he was always conspicuous. Not one in the school could compete with him in long-distance running, and when he was one of the hares there was but little chance for the hounds. He was a capital swimmer and one of the best boxers in the school. He had a reputation for being a leader in every mischievous prank; but he was honourable and manly, would scorn to shelter himself under the semblance of a lie, and was a prime favourite with his masters as well as his schoolfellows.

G. A. Henty, *With Clive in India; or, The Beginnings of an Empire* (1884), p. 11

The fully-fledged Henty hero, it has been said, was an abstraction of pluck, physical endurance and honour, the qualities which supposedly had built the British empire.

In this way Henty's adventure stories instilled and re-inforced a set of upper-middle-class social views and values. Henty preached British superiority and the white man's duty towards inferior races. His readers were encouraged not only to admire and emulate the hero but to view the empire as a vehicle for self-fulfilment, fulfilling the British race's divine mission to civilize and to govern a large part of humanity. His 'natives' both welcomed and legitimised British rule, even justifying the former system of slavery:

Me trabel a good deal, and me tink dat no working people in de world so merry and happy as de slabe in a plantation wid a good massa and missy. Dey not work so hard as de white man. Dey have plenty to eat and drink, dey habe deir gardens and deir fowls. When dey are sick dey are taken care ob, when dey are ole they are looked after and hab nothing to do. I have heard people talk a lot of nonsense about de hard life of de plantation slabe. Dat not true, sar, wid a good massa. De slabe hab no care and he bery happy. If de massas were good, and dere were a law dat if a plantation were broken up de slabes must be sold in families together, me tell you dat de life on a plantation a thousand times happer dan de life ob de black man in his own country.

G. A. Henty, *By Sheer Pluck* (1884), p. 185

Clearly, it was Britain's *duty* to rule. The British empire was the greatest force for good the world had ever seen.

With Haggard and Conrad into the Unknown

While Henty wrote adventure stories for boys about boys who usually acted like grown men, Rider Haggard wrote mainly for an adult audience about men who frequently reverted to being boys. Not surprisingly Haggard's romances soon became popular with a juvenile audience.

Haggard wrote a whole series of 'ripping yarns', the most well known being those set in Africa: *King Solomon's Mines* written in six weeks in 1885 as the result of a bet with his brother that he could outdo Stevenson's *Treasure Island*, *Allan Quatermain* (1887), *She* (1887), *Nada the Lily* (1892) and *Ayesha* (1905). Many of his stories concerned the history of the Zulus, the subject of his first non-fiction work, *Cetewayo and His White Neighbours* (1881). His best remembered romances, however, deal with imaginary peoples and fantasy landscapes and play on the popular ideas and imagination of the age.

In *King Solomon's Mines*, three white men, Allan Quatermain (probably based on the African hunter Frederick Courtney Selous), a young aristocrat Sir Henry Curtis, and a very English naval officer Captain Good, accompanied by a proud and intelligent African, set off in search of Curtis' lost brother and the fabled diamond mines of King Solomon marked on a faded Portuguese map. On the way they encounter big game, scorching deserts, frozen mountains, and experience starvation before arriving in Kukuanaland, a pastoral paradise, occupied by a Zulu-speaking people living amid the stone ruins of a long-vanished civilization. When the trio fall foul of the tyrannical ruler by saving a beautiful maiden from sacrifice, their African companion reveals himself as the rightful king. A bloody battle ensues in which Sir Henry appears dressed in leopard skins and ostrich feathers ferociously wielding a battle axe like his Viking ancestors:

> There he stood, the great Dane, for he was nothing else, his hands, his axe, and his armour all red with blood, and none could live before his stroke. Time after time I saw it sweeping down, as some great warrior ventured to give him battle, and as he struck he shouted 'O-hoy! O-hoy!' like his Berserker forefathers, and the blow went crashing through shield and spear, through head dress, hair and skull.

H. Rider Haggard, *King Solomon's Mines* (1885), p. 150

After victory has been attained the grateful Ignosi forces the old witch, Gagool, to lead the white men to the hiding place of the diamonds. Gagool traps the trio in the treasure cave but is herself killed by the young maiden. The white men escape through subterranean caverns eventually returning to England with their booty having found the long lost brother on the way.

In *Allan Quatermain*, the trio return to the centre of Africa, this time accompanied by a magnificent Zulu, Umslopogaas, in search of a lost white civilization. After the usual adventures and a ferocious battle with the Masai, the party travels along a subterranean river and enters Zu-Vendis, a medieval world of chivalry and courtly love, ruled over by a light-skinned aristocracy and a superstitious priesthood. Following tensions between the state and church and a quarrel between the sister queens over the handsome Sir Henry, civil war breaks out and an even more ferocious battle ensues. Finally, Curtis decides to remain in Zu-Vendis with the intention of excluding all foreigners:

> I am convinced of the sacred duty that rests upon me of preserving to this, on the whole, upright and generous-hearted people the blessing of comparative barbarism [. . . .] I have no fancy for handing over

this beautiful country to be torn and fought for by speculators, tourists, politicians and teachers, whose voice is as the voice of Babel [. . . .] Nor will I endow it with the greed, drunkenness, new diseases, gunpowder, and general demoralisation which chiefly mark the progress of civilization amongst unsophisticated peoples.

H. Rider Haggard, *Allan Quatermain* (1887), pp. 276–7

Despite the surprising conclusion, it is possible to see why such stories had so much appeal for an impressionable audience. The imperial romance provided excitement and an outlet for an increasingly militaristic British public. In *Nada the Lily*, described in one magazine as 'drenched, sodden, dripping with blood', a vivid Zulu description of war expressed feelings not often reflected in English literature:

Ah, the battle! – the battle! In those days we knew how to fight, my father! All night our fires shone out across the valley; all night the songs of soldiers echoed down the hills. Then the grey dawning came, the oxen lowed to the light, the regiments rose from their bed of spears; they sprang up and shook the dew from their hair and shields – yes! They arose! The glad to die! [. . .] The morning breeze came up and found them, their plumes bent in the breeze; like a plain of seeding grass they bent, the plumes of soldiers ripe for the assegai. Up over the shoulder of the hill came the sun of Slaughter; it glowed red upon the red shields; red grew the place of killing; the white plumes of chiefs were dipped in the blood of heaven. They knew it; they saw the omen of death, and, ah! they laughed in the joy of the waking battle. What was death? Was it not well to die on the spear? What was death? Was it not well to die for the king? Death was the arms of Victory. Victory should be their bride that night, and ah! her breast is fair.

H. Rider Haggard, *Nada the Lily* (1892), pp. 48–9

It is easy to see why these romances were popular as Sunday school and school prizes, perhaps a little less easy to see why they were given.

For adults, however, the novels had a wider fascination. In the age of social Darwinism, they could be read on a deeper level. Africa is the primitive past, the African is the white-man's former savage self – and the barbarian in the inner being can surface again if the conditions are right. Thus as the adventurers thrust deeper into Africa they undergo physical and moral tests which gradually strip away the veneer of civilization, the many layers of personality, until in a bloody climax they finally go beserk possessed of 'a savage desire to kill and spare not'. Sir Henry Curtis appears dressed in the same way as Ignosi and fights as savagely. In the heart of Africa there is no God and no moral law. The inner, black, uncivilized self is revealed as well as the ancient self representing earlier stages in European civilization – the Vikings and the medieval knights of feudal England. Allan Quatermain philosophises:

> Ah! this civilization, what does it all come to? Full forty years and more I spent among savages, and studied them and their nature; and now for several years I have lived here in England, and in my own stupid manner have done my best to learn the ways of the children of light; and what do I find? A great gulf fixed? No, only a very little one [. . . .] Civilization is only savagery silver-gilt [. . . .]
>
> This being so, supposing for the sake of argument that we divide our identities into twenty parts, nineteen savage and one civilized, we must look to the nineteen savage portions, if we would really understand ourselves, and not to the twentieth, which, though so insignificant in reality, is spread all over the other nineteen, making them appear quite different from what they really are, as the blacking does a boot, or the veneer a table. It is on the nineteen rough, serviceable, savage portions that we fall back in emergencies, not on the polished but unsubstantial twentieth. Civilization should wipe away our tears, and yet we weep and cannot be comforted. Warfare

is abhorrent to her, and yet we strike out for hearth and home, for honour and fair fame, and can glory in the blow. And so on, through everything.

.So, when the heart is stricken, and the head is humbled in the dust, civilization fails us utterly.

H. Rider Haggard, *Allan Quatermain* (1887), pp. 4–6

It is this fear of a reversion to barbarism that Haggard explores so vividly. Stevenson's *The Strange Case of Dr. Jekyll and Mr. Hyde* (1886) also examines, in an urban setting, the release of the primitive, ape-like natural man living beneath the civilized skin, a phenomenon explored in different ways in Oscar Wilde's *The Picture of Dorian Gray* (1890) and Bram Stoker's *Dracula* (1897). No wonder the British meticulously dressed for dinner in the middle of the jungle.

Joseph Conrad in *Heart of Darkness* (1902) traces the result of betraying the ideals of civilization to its terrifying conclusion. The noble and idealistic Kurtz situated in darkest Africa submits to alcohol, isolation and megalomania and ends up radiating darkness, the high priest of a primitive tribe practising unspeakable rites. Marlow relates that at the moment of Kurtz's death:

> Anything approaching the change that came over his features I have never seen before, and hope never to see again [. . . .] It was as though a veil had been rent. I saw on that ivory face the expression of sombre pride, of ruthless power, of craven terror – of an intense and hopeless despair. Did he live his life again in every detail of desire, temptation, and surrender during that supreme moment of complete knowledge? He cried in a whisper at some image, at some vision – he cried out twice, a cry that was no more than a breath: 'The horror! The horror!'.

J. Conrad, *Heart of Darkness* (1902), p. 84

But, despite the horror, for Conrad the excitement had gone out of adventure. Arriving at Stanley Falls in 1890, he noted a great melancholy. Instead of a great haunting memory, only the unholy recollection of a prosaic newspaper 'stunt' and the distasteful knowledge of the vilest scramble for loot that ever disfigured the history of human conscience and geographical exploration. What an end to the idealized realities of a boy's daydreams!

J. Conrad, 'Geography and Some Explorers' in *Last Essays* (1926), p. 17

Heart of Darkness was both a romance and an exposé of King Leopold's imperialism. Like the Eldorado Exploring Expedition:

it was reckless without hardihood, greedy without audacity, and cruel without courage [. . . .] To tear treasure out of the bowels of the earth was their desire, with no more moral purpose at the back of it than there is in burglars breaking into a safe.

J. Conrad, *Heart of Darkness* (1902), p. 35

Conrad was sceptical about the part played by the spirit of adventure in fuelling the New Imperialism:

The mere love of adventure is no saving grace. It is no grace at all. It lays a man under no obligation to faithfulness to an idea and even to his own self [. . . .] There is nothing in the world to prevent a mere lover or pursuer of adventure from running at any moment [. . . .] You find them in mysterious nooks of islands and continents, mostly red-nosed and watery-eyed, and not even amusingly boastful. There is nothing more futile [. . . .] Adventure by itself is but a phantom, a dubious shape without a heart.

J. Conrad, 'Well Done' (1918) in *Notes on Life and Letters* (1921), pp. 255–6

For Conrad, the adventure of imperialism had lost both intellectual and moral credibility.

In the early twentieth century it was Conrad, not Kipling, who was accepted into the English literary tradition. After Forster's *A Passage to India* (1924) and Somerset Maugham's series of stories, those who continued to use the adventure genre in an imperial setting – George Orwell, Joyce Cary, Evelyn Waugh and Graham Greene – used it sardonically. It became the fashion to mock both the adventurer and the empire. But the imperial romance was by no means dead. The imperial adventure story continued to flourish and have an impact outside the confines of those works formally dubbed 'English Literature'. John Buchan, a craftsman in the Stevenson mould, was one of the more popular writers. His *Prester John* (1910) contained all the ingredients of a Haggard romance. The genre was kept alive by A. E. W. Mason, Edgar Wallace, Edgar Rice Burroughs and W. E. Johns. The mid-Victorian classics continued to be read, as did Henty and Rider Haggard. The 1930s witnessed the popular screening of, among others, *King Solomon's Mines*, *The Four Feathers* and *Sanders of the River*, along with Mason's novella *The Drum* (1938). For boys, the *Gem* and *Magnet* were replaced by *Rover*, *Wizard* and *Hotspur*. Juvenile literature stuck to its traditional form: public school stories, science fiction, spy stories, imperial adventure and the reliving of colonial campaigns, well into the 1950s. All Henty's titles were still in print in 1955 and many were later reprinted, though frequently in abridged form. The energising myths of empire remained at the heart of popular culture decades after high culture had abandoned them. Xenophobia and national and racial superiority lived on in children's literature.

The imperial adventure genre, then, played an important role in popularising and glamourising the empire. The empire became a place of romance and adventure with its centre in the dark continent. It had its most enduring form of expression in popular culture, thus making the working classes more aware of the empire's existence. The imperial romance and the empire adventure story not only roused public excitement and interest in the tropics, they helped to confirm and to disseminate the late-Victorian world-view.

3   By Jingo!

> There is an universal scramble for plunder, for ex-
> citement, for amusement, for speculation, and above
> it all the flag of a Hooligan Imperialism is raised,
> with the proclamation that it is the sole mission of
> Anglo-Saxon England, forgetful of the task of keep-
> ing its own drains in order, to expand and extend its
> boundaries indefinitely, and, again in the name of
> Christianity it has practically abandoned, to conquer
> and inherit the Earth.
>
> R. Buchanan, 'The Voice of the Hooligan', *Contemporary
> Review* (December 1899), in R. Koebner & H. D. Schmidt,
> *Imperialism: the Story and Significance of a Political Word,
> 1840–1960* (1964), p. 229

By the late 1880s, British public interest in the colonies had
increased dramatically. The explorations in Africa, the death
of Livingstone, the discovery of gold and diamonds, Disraeli's creation of the Queen as Empress of India and his
revelling in British rule overseas, the various 'little wars' of
the 1870s and 1880s and the jingoistic outbursts which accompanied them, as well as the new racial theories which
were gradually beginning to capture the public imagination,
had all played their part. There were also mounting fears
about Great Britain's economic prospects and growing concern about her future role in the world, with new rivals
showing an interest in colonial expansion as Great Britain
became increasingly isolated. Britain's knee-jerk responses,
the acquisition of more territory and the chauvinism of the
late 1890s, were as much the product of these feelings of
insecurity as they were of arrogance and pride.

Perhaps the change in tone and style of the age can best
be illustrated by contrasting the content of Sir John Seeley's Cambridge lectures on *The Expansion of England*,

delivered in 1881–2, with the impassioned lectures on Great Britain's world mission delivered by Professor J. A. Cramb at Queen's College, London University, during the Boer War:

> Every year, every month that passes, is fraught with import of the high and singular destiny which awaits this realm, this empire and this race [. . . .] And lo! gathering up from the elder centuries, a sound like a trumpet call, clear-piercing, far-borne, mystic, ineffable, the call to battle of hosts invisible, the mustering armies of the dead, the great of other wars Brunanburh and Senlac, Creçy, Flodden, Blenheim and Trafalgar. *Their* battle-cries await our answer – the chivalry's at Agincourt, 'Heaven for Harry, England and St George!', Cromwell's war shout, which was a prayer at Dunbar, 'The Lord of Hosts, The Lord of Hosts!' – these await our answer, that response which by this war we at last send ringing down the ages, 'God for Britain, Justice and Freedom to the world!'
>
> With us, let me repeat, the decision rests, with us and with this generation. Never since on Sinai God spoke in thunder has mandate more imperative been issued to any race, city, or nation than now to this nation and to this people. And, again, if we should hesitate, or if we should decide wrongly, it is not the loss of prestige, it is not the narrowed bounds we have to fear, it is the judgment of the dead and the despair of the living, of the inarticulate myriads who have trusted to us, it is the arraigning eyes of the unborn.
>
> J. A. Cramb, *The Origins and Destiny of Imperial Britain* (1915), pp. 224, 226

By the end of the nineteenth century British patriotism had taken on a much harder cutting edge. In many ways it was a perverted patriotism based on ideas of Anglo-Saxon 'manifest destiny', race-pride and social Darwinism, combined with monarchism and a growing militarism – the worship of power and force and the glorification of war.

An Increasing Belligerence

> We don't want to fight, but by jingo if we do,
> We've got the ships, we've got the men, we've got the
>   money too.
> We've fought the Bear before, and while we're
>   Britons true,
> The Russians shall not have Constantinople.

> G. W. Hunt, 'By Jingo' or 'The Dogs of War', 1877

G. W. Hunt's war song, performed in the music halls by G.
H. Macdermott during the Eastern Question crisis of 1877–8,
is usually credited with having added the word 'jingoism' to
the English vocabulary. Such outbursts of xenophobia were
not uncommon, especially at times of national crisis. Another
such occasion was the 'martyrdom' of General Gordon in
1885 when the relief column, belatedly despatched by the
Gladstone government, arrived at Khartoum two days after
Gordon's death. Queen and country were furious. Gladstone, who had been heavily criticised for the ignominious
end to the first Boer War (Gerald Manley Hopkins, an un-
equivocal patriot, loathed Gladstone and despised a nation
which 'gapes on while Gladstone negotiates his surrenders of
empire'), found himself the subject of another bitter attack:

> A skilful leech, so long as we were whole:
> Who scanned the nation's every outward part
> But ah! misheard the beating of its heart.
> Sire of huge sorrows, yet erect of soul.
> Swift rider with calamity for goal,
> Who, overtasking his equestrian art,
> Unstall'd a steed full willing for the start,
> But wondrous hard to curb or control.
> Sometimes we thought he led the people forth:
> Anon he seemed to follow where they flew:
> Lord of the golden tongue and smiting eyes;
> Great out of season and untimely wise:
> A man whose virtue, genius, grandeur, worth,
> Wrought deadlier ill than ages can undo.

> Sir William Watson, 'Gladstone' (1885), ll. 1–14

Tennyson's verse was also becoming noticeably patriotic:

> Sharers of our glorious past,
> Brothers, must we part at last?
> Shall we not through good and ill
> Cleave to one another still?
> Britain's myriad voices call,
> 'Sons, be welded each and all,
> Into one imperial whole,
> One with Britain, heart and soul!
> One life, one flag, one fleet, one Throne!'
>   Britons, hold your own!

Lord Tennyson, 'Opening of the Indian and Colonial Exhibition by the Queen' (1886), ll. 31–40

And, on the occasion of the Queen's Golden Jubilee:

> Fifty years of ever-broadening Commerce!
> Fifty years of ever-brightening Science!
> Fifty years of ever-broadening Empire!
>
> You, the Mighty, the Fortunate,
> You, the Lord-territorial,
> You, the Lord-manufacturer,
> You, the hardy, laborious,
> Patient children of Albion,
> You, Canadian, Indian,
> Australasian, African,
> All your hearts be in harmony,
> All your voices in unison,
> Singing 'Hail to the glorious
> Golden year of her Jubilee!'

Lord Tennyson, 'On the Jubilee of Queen Victoria' (1887), ll. 52–65

The poetry of patriotism became increasingly insensitive. W. E. Henley, who led a literary counter-movement against the late nineteenth-century 'decadents', gloried in the less pleasant aspects of Britain's rule:

They call you proud and hard,
   England, my England:
You with worlds to watch and ward,
   England, my own!
You whose mailed hand keeps the keys
   Of such teeming destinies,
You could know nor dread nor ease,
   Were the Song of your bugles blown,
      England –
Round the Pit on your bugles blown!

W. E. Henley, 'Pro Rege Nostro' (1892), ll. 31–40

The nadir of poetic jingoism was surely reached when, after an interval of four years, Tennyson was succeeded as Poet Laureate by the journalist Alfred Austin. Alfred the Great was followed by Alfred the Little ran a contemporary joke. His first official utterance, ten days after his appointment, appeared in *The Times* on 11 January 1896 – to the annoyance of the Queen and the embarrassment of her Prime Minister. It concerned Dr Leander Starr Jameson's ill-advised 'raid' into the Transvaal with 600 men at the time of an intended Uitlander uprising, an act rapidly disowned by Lord Salisbury:

Wrong! Is it wrong? Well, may be
But I'm going, boys, all the same.
Do they think me a Burgher's baby,
To be scared by a scolding name?
They may argue, and prate, and order;
Go, tell them to save their breath:
Then, over the Transvaal border,
And gallop for life or death!

Let lawyers and statesmen addle
Their pates over points of law:
If sound be our sword and saddle
And gun-gear, who cares one straw?
When men of our own blood pray us
To ride to their kinsfolk's aid,
Not heaven itself shall stay us
From the rescue they call a raid.

There are girls in the gold-reef city,
There are mothers and children too!
And they cry, 'Hurry up! for pity.'
So what can a brave man do?
If ever we win, they'll blame us:
If we fail, they will howl and hiss.
But there's many a man lives famous
For daring a wrong like this!

[. . .]

I suppose we were wrong, were mad-
    men,
Still I think at the Judgment day,
When God sifts the good from the bad
    men,
They'll be something more to say.
We were wrong but we aren't half
    sorry,
And, as one of the baffled band,
I would rather have had that foray
Than the crushings of all the Rand.

A. Austin, 'Jameson's Ride', *The Times*, 11 January 1896

In fact, many contemporaries agreed with the 'Hysterical Helot of Imperialism'. Alfred Edgar, the editor of *Pluck*, recorded:

All Britain has been aroused by the extraordinary transactions that have recently occurred in the Transvaal, and the trumpets of war, at the time we write, may at any moment give forth such a blast as shall gather together all who cherish the cause of justice and honour to do battle on its behalf.

Whatever may be said of Dr. Jameson's particular movement in Johannesburg, he has given us one of the most remarkable exhibitions of British pluck on record [. . . .] The story of Krugersdorp and Vlak-fontein is one for England to be proud of, whatever

the wisdom of the cause may have been – and we
have yet to find proof that it was not the glorious
cause of Englishmen fighting to save the lives of their
endangered countrymen.
History shows us no more splendid page of heroism struggling against tremendous odds [. . . .]

A. Edgar, 'The Editor's Weekly Word', *Pluck*,
24 January 1896, Vol. 3, No. 62, p. 16

Clement Attlee, the future Labour Prime Minister, later recalled how his father, a Gladstonian Liberal, had been
shocked by Jameson's action,

but to us Dr. Jim was a hero [. . . .] On the wall at
school hung a great map with large portions of it
coloured red. It was an intoxicating vision for a small
boy [. . . .] We believed in our great imperial mission

C. R. Attlee, *Empire into Commonwealth* (1961),
pp. 5–6

In similar fashion, Rider Haggard lauded the crushing of
King Lobengula's armies in Matabeleland by Rhodes' British South Africa Company. It was for the good of the world
that Englishmen should dominate in Africa. He knew some
would regard it as vulgar:

That was rank Jingoism – his sin was ever before him:
but all the same while he had a voice to speak, a pen
to write, or any power to move the hearts of men, he
meant to go on sinning thus, for to him the English
name was the most glorious in history, and the English flag the most splendid that ever flew above the
peoples of the earth.

H. Rider Haggard, speech to the Anglo-African
Writers' Club, *Pall Mall Gazette*, 24 April 1894, p. 8

In 1898, even Lord Salisbury divided the nations of the
world into 'living' and 'dying' states, predicting:

For one reason or another – from the necessities of politics or under the pretence of philanthropy, the living nations will gradually encroach on the territory of the dying, and the seeds and causes of conflict among civilized nations will speedily appear.

Marquis of Salisbury, speech to the Primrose League, 4 May 1898, *The Times*, 5 May 1898

By May 1899, Joseph Chamberlain was convinced that the Boers' turn had come. Lord Milner insisted that some show of strength was essential:

The spectacle of thousands of British subjects kept permanently in the position of helots, constantly chafing under undoubted grievances, and calling vainly to Her Majesty's Government for redress does steadily undermine the influence and reputation of Great Britain and the respect for the British Government within the Queen's dominions [. . . .] The best proof of its power and its justice would be to obtain for the Uitlanders of the Transvaal a fair share in the government of a country which owes everything to their exertions.

Lord Milner, May 1899, in Headlam, *Milner Papers*, Vol. II, pp. 352–3

The temper of the times was certainly shown the day following the receipt of the Boer ultimatum in October 1899 when Algernon Swinburne sallied forth with:

Speech and song
Lack utterance now for loathing. Scarce we hear
  Foul tongues that blacken God's dishonoured
    name
  With prayers turned curses and with praise found
    shame
Defy the truth whose witness now draws near

To scourge these dogs, agape with jaws afoam,
Down out of life. Strike, England, and strike home.

> A. C. Swinburne, 'The Transvaal' (1899), ll. 8–14

England did not live up to expectations. W. E. Henley was 'knocked speechless with wrath and amazement' by the British reverses at Stormberg, Magersfontein and Colenso during 'Black Week', December 1899:

Hitch, blunder, check –
  Each is a *new disaster*,
And it is who shall bleat and scrawl
  The feebler and the faster.
Where is our ancient pride of heart?
  Our faith in blood and star?
Who but would marvel how we came
  If this is all we are?

Ours is the race
  That tore the Spaniard's ruff,
That flung the Dutchman by the breech,
  The Frenchman by the scruff;
Through his diurnal round of dawns
  Our drum-tap squires the sun;
And yet, an old mad burgher man
  Can put us on the run!

> W. E. Henley, 'Remonstrance' (1899), ll. 1–16

When the tide of events turned in Britain's favour in 1900, following the arrival of Lord Roberts, Henley gloated over Boer misfortunes:

By the dismal fords, the thankless hills, the desolate,
    half-dead flats
He has shepherded them like silly sheep, and
    cornered them like rats.
He has driven and herded them strength by strength,
    as a hunter deals with his deer,

And has filled the place of the heart in their breast
with a living devil of fear.

W. E. Henley, 'Our Chief of Men' (1900),
ll. 17–24

The near hysteria which accompanied the reliefs of Kimberley, Ladysmith and Mafeking was typical of the age:

> Would the critics of 'music hall madness' prefer to
> see a city stand sullen, silent, indifferent, cursing in
> the bitterness of its heart the government, the army,
> the empire? Or would they have it like the Roman
> mob of the first Caesars, cluster in crowds, careless
> of empire, battles or the glory of Rome's name,
> shouting for a loaf of bread or a circus ticket?

J. A. Cramb, *Reflections on The Origins and Destiny of
Imperial Britain* (1900), p. 107

asked Professor Cramb. The hatred with which Britain was
viewed in the rest of Europe was the result of *phthonos*,
Immortal Envy. War, he declared, was not the destruction
but the intensification of life, a means of self-fulfilment for
the ordinary British soldier:

> There is nothing in our annals which warrants evil
> pressage from the spread of militarism [. . . .] The
> battlefield is an altar [. . . .] Fighting for ideal ends,
> he dies, knowing in his heart that they may never
> be at all. Courage and self-renunciation have at-
> tained their height.

Ibid, pp. 110, 148–9

Cramb's account of the origins of the Boer War, and the
glory of war, met their sharpest rebuke (and the exponents
of jingoism their comeuppance) with the publication of J. A.
Hobson's *Imperialism, A Study* (1902). From that time on,
the word 'imperialism' entered on a new Continental career.
It was used to describe an inflated and arrogant form of

English nationalism. In Great Britain, the critics of imperialism now girded their loins, while its defenders sought desperately to dissociate imperialism from the objectionable features of jingoism. It was an uphill task.

The Education of the Boyish Masters

> Most serious of all is the persistent attempt to seize the school system for Imperialism masquerading as patriotism. To capture the childhood of the country, to mechanize its free play into the routine of military drill, to cultivate the savage survivals of combativeness, to poison its early understanding of history by false ideals and pseudo-heroes, and by a consequent disparagement and neglect of the really vital and elevating lessons of the past, to establish a 'geocentric' view of the moral universe in which the interests of humanity are subordinate to that of the 'country' [. . .] to feed the always overweening pride of race at an age when self confidence most commonly prevails, and by necessary implication to disparage other nations, so starting children in the world with false measures of value and an unwillingness to learn from foreign sources – to fasten this base insularity of mind and morals upon the little children of a nation and to call it patriotism is as foul an abuse of education as it is possible to conceive.
>
> J. A. Hobson, *Imperialism, A Study* (1902), pp. 229–30

According to Hobson, the English had a misplaced reverence for their imperial patrimony instilled into them virtually from the cradle.

One of the most tireless imperial propagandists, the twelfth Earl of Meath (who successfully campaigned for the introduction of annual 'Empire Day' celebrations), certainly believed:

> In former ages the burdens of Empire or of the State fell on the shoulders of a few; now the humblest child to be found on the benches of a primary school will

in a few years be called on to influence the destinies not only of fifty-four millions of whites, but of three hundred and fifty millions of coloured men and women, his fellow subjects, scattered throughout the five continents of the world.

Earl of Meath, 'Duty and discipline in the training of children', *Essays on Duty and Discipline* (1911), p. 59

In Edwardian Salford, Robert Roberts later recalled:

Teachers fed on Seeley's imperialistic work *The Expansion of England*, and often great readers of Kipling, spelled out patriotism among us [. . .] with a fervour that with some edged on the religious.

R. Roberts, *The Classic Slum* (1971) p. 112

Most schools had large maps of the world on Mercator's projection with the British colonies marked in a vivid red. Reproductions of patriotic or military scenes, perhaps one of Lady Butler's paintings or a Caton Woodville, typically adorned the walls. Successive Elementary School Codes and manuals for teachers placed increasing emphasis on the study of the empire. Gradually the curriculum and textbooks became more imperially slanted and military drill was even included as an 'alternative' activity in the Elementary School Code of 1871. History, geography and English were the subjects most used to instil patriotism, militarism, adulation of the monarchy and imperial values. In history textbooks, awkward events were skirted round, British misdeeds ignored, and moral responsibility for conflict consistently shifted onto the shoulders of others. One of the most popular propagandist books was C. R. Fletcher and Rudyard Kipling's *School History of England*, with stirring verses supplied by the latter. Geography texts were particularly adept at conveying social Darwinian ideas. Even English 'readers' conveyed similar sentiments, being heavily dependent on travel, military, missionary and adventure stories. In this manner one generation conveyed the dominant ideology to the next. Attlee's recollection that in 1897 'most of us boys were imperialists' was endorsed by the novelist Frank Bullen in 1902:

> No one would dare enter a [...] school in this country and speak against the Empire. Did he do so, he would be knocked down.
>
> F. Bullen, 'Supplement', *Boys of Our Empire*,
> 6 December 1902, No. 3, p. iv

What was true of State schools was even more true of the private sector. The public schools were the nursery of empire. From the 1850s, their whole ethos – fagging, the prefect system, the cult of athleticism, the house, spartan living conditions – was geared to instilling group and institutional loyalty, obedience, 'manliness', self-control, resourcefulness, the ability to command, all the qualities essential to a ruling race capable of surviving in imperial climes. In short, the training of 'character' took precedence over intellectual studies. As one headmaster, the Rev. T. C. Papillon, claimed, the public school boy's scholastic shortcomings were more than compensated for by his other qualities:

> Many a lad who leaves an English public school disgracefully ignorant of the rudiments of useful knowledge, and who can speak no language but his own, and writes that imperfectly, to whom the noble literature of his country and the stirring history of his forefathers are almost a sealed book, and who has devoted a great part of his time and nearly all his thoughts to athletic sports, yet brings away with him something beyond all price, a manly straightforward character, a scorn of lying and meanness, habits of obedience and command, and fearless courage. Thus equipped, he goes out into the world and bears a man's part in subduing the earth, ruling its wild folk, and building up the Empire.
>
> T. C. Papillon, quoted in B. Darwin, *The English Public School* (1929), p. 21

Sir Henry Newbolt's poems 'Clifton Chapel' and 'Vitaï

Lampada' convey the ethos of these schools. G. A. Henty certainly preferred the lad who could ride and shoot to a boy who could quote Euripides or solve problems in higher mathematics. Thomas Hughes likewise could forgive a boy's ignorance of digamma and Greek particles so long as he 'played the game'. As J. E. C. Welldon, the headmaster of Harrow, put it:

> Englishmen are not superior to Frenchmen or Germans in brains or industry or the science and apparatus of war; but they are superior in the health and temper which games impart [. . . .] I do not think that I am wrong in saying that the sport, the pluck, the resolution, and the strength which have within the last few weeks animated the little garrison at Chitral and the gallant force that has accomplished their deliverance are effectively acquired in the cricket fields and football fields of the great public schools, and in the games of which they are the habitual scenes. The pluck, the energy, the perseverance, the good temper, the self-control, the discipline, the cooperation, the *esprit de corps*, which merit success in cricket or football, are the very qualities which win the day in peace or war. The men who possessed these qualities, not sedate and faultless citizens, but men of will, spirit, and chivalry, are the men who conquered at Plassey and Quebec. In the history of the British Empire it is written that England has owed her sovereignty to her sports.

J. E. C. Welldon, 'The imperial purpose of education', *Proceedings of the Royal Colonial Institute* (1894–5), Vol. 26, p. 829

It was a banal argument, but it was widely accepted. Other headmasters – Warre of Eton, Rendall of Winchester, Almond of Loretto, Norwood of Marlborough, Thring of Uppingham – and their staffs were equally forceful propagators of imperialism, spreading their influence through chapel sermons, Speech Day addresses, school magazines, the Cadet Corps, as well as through the curriculum and on the sports field. The buildings themselves were full of imperial reminders: at Sedbergh the chapel contained a stained glass window with three panels commemorating Sir John Lawrence, General Gordon and Bishop Patteson of Melanesia. Welldon concluded:

> The boys of today are the statesmen and administrators of to-morrow. In their hands is the future of the British Empire. May they prove themselves not unworthy of their solemn charge! May they scorn the idea of tarnishing or diminishing the Empire which their forefathers won! May they augment, consolidate, and exalt it! May it be given them to cherish great ideas, to make great efforts, and to win great victories! That is my prayer.

Ibid, p. 839

The indoctrination of imperial ideas was not restricted to the schoolroom. Sometimes leisure hours were spent in overtly imperialist organisations such as Howard Spicer's Boys' Empire League, dedicated to the ideals of Christian manliness and patriotism. The foundation of William Smith's Boys' Brigade in 1883 and Walter Gee's Anglican Church Lads' Brigade in 1891 marked the increasing militarism of the age. Significantly, 'Fight the Good Fight', 'Onward Christian Soldiers' and 'Stand up, stand up for Jesus, ye soldiers of the Cross' were among the most popular hymns of the day. The same period saw the foundation of the Salvation Army and the Church Army, and even workers in the Post Office and on the railways were put into uniform. Perhaps military and imperial ideals were most closely welded together in Baden-Powell's Boy Scout (and his sister's Girl Guide) movement. The 'wolf cub' packs were based on Kipling's *Jungle Books* and Kipling also contributed the official Boy Scout song. B-P's *Scouting for Boys: A Handbook for Instruction in Good Citizenship* (his sister also wrote a book on *How Girls Can Help Build Up the Empire*) was full of imperial and patriotic ideals.

[. . .] don't be disgraced like the young Romans, who

lost the Empire of their forefathers by being wishy-washy slackers without any go or patriotism in them. Play up! Each man in his place, and play the game! Your fathers worked hard, fought hard, and died hard, to make this Empire for you. Don't let them look down from heaven, and see you loafing about with hands in your pockets doing nothing to keep it up.

Robert Baden-Powell, *Scouting for Boys* (1908), p. 267

There were sections on 'Patriotism', 'How our Empire Grew' and 'How the Empire must be Held'. *Scouting for Boys* became an international best-seller and the Scout movement one of the most successful youth movements of all time. The youth of England in the late Victorian and Edwardian years were clearly brought up in an atmostphere pervaded by imperial values and patriotic sentiments.

The Popularisation of Empire

While a number of formal organisations and events – the Royal Empire Society, the Colonial and Indian Exhibition of 1886, the Imperial Institute, the Imperial Federation League, the Primrose League, the Victoria League, and the acceptance in 1903 of an official Empire Day – provided imperial propaganda in the late nineteenth and early twentieth centuries, they were generally less successful than the media in the promotion of empire. If the constant stream of hero-worshipping popular lives of imperial and military figures, with their stirring titles, imaginative dust-jackets and exciting cover illustrations failed to achieve an impact, few could have missed the products of the mushrooming advertising industry. Tea, tobacco, chocolate, soap and biscuit companies, in particular, packaged their wares in tins and boxes covered with empire scenes and familiar figures of military and imperial renown. Apparently, the Boer War might have ended much sooner if British soldiers had spent less time waving cigarette packets from the tops of hills. Indeed, if one Bovril advertisement is to be believed, Lord Roberts' route

across the Orange Free State carefully spelt out the word
'Bovril'. A vast number of postcards and cigarette cards
depicting the empire were also produced: pictures of imperial heroes, military uniforms, empire flags, imperial products and industries, were churned out in their thousands.
The issue of commemorative ware – mugs, plates, jugs – on
royal occasions and at other times of celebration ensured an
ever widening distribution of patriotic and imperial images.
With the Victorian craze for bric-à-brac the empire was
further exploited for commercial profit.

This tremendous growth in advertising was, in part, the
result of the growth in newspapers and popular journals. An
attempt by W. T. Stead in the *Pall Mall Gazette* to break
away from the old-style densely packed columns of news-
print and dull reporting of parliamentary debates, was over-
shadowed in 1896 by the appearance of Alfred
Harmsworth's halfpenny *Daily Mail*, which stood, Harmsworth wrote,

> for the power, the supremacy and the greatness of
> the British Empire [. . . .] The *Daily Mail* is the em-
> bodiment and the mouthpiece of the imperial idea.
> Those who launched this journal had one definite
> aim in view [. . .] to be the articulate voice of British
> progress and domination. We believe in England. We
> know that the advance of the Union Jack means pro-
> tection for weaker races, justice for the oppressed,
> liberty for the down-trodden. Our Empire has not
> exhausted itself.
>
> W. L. Langer, *The Diplomacy of Imperialism,*
> *1890–1902* (1965), p. 84

Lord Salisbury at first dismissed this mouthpiece of the New
Imperialism as catering for those who could read but could
not think. However, the *Mail*'s circulation reached the unprecedented figure of 1 000 000 in 1901. Its appearance was
followed by the foundation of the equally strident *Daily
Express* in 1900 and the *Standard of Empire* in 1908. While
the people who mattered continued to read the older style
newspapers, it soon became noticeable that *The Times* was

becoming as vigorously imperialistic in tone as *The Ob-server* under J. L. Garvin's editorship.

Newspapers played a crucial role in publicising and popu-larising the empire in the late nineteenth century. After the success of W. H. Russell's despatches during the Crimean War, readers eagerly consumed news of the imperial cam-paigns which seemed to occur annually throughout Queen Victoria's reign. The first 'little war' to receive full coverage was the Abyssinian expedition of 1867. The British army was accompanied by a whole posse of 'special correspond-ents', including H. M. Stanley and G. A. Henty, and, for the first time, an official photographic unit was attached to the Royal Engineers. Henty, Stanley, Archibald Forbes, Edgar Wallace and G. W. Steevens became household names as they whetted the public appetite with their stories of der-ring-do. Their sensational fare provided suitable entertain-ment for a distant, semi-literate reading public.

> You're sent out when a war begins, to minister to the blind, brutal, British public's bestial thirst for blood
>
> R. Kipling, *The Light That Failed* (1890), p. 51

accuses a character in Rudyard Kipling's first novel *The Light That Failed*. According to Kipling:

> The Sudan campaign was a picturesque one, and lent itself to vivid word painting. Now and again a 'spe-cial' managed to get slain – which was not altogether a disadvantage to the paper that employed him – and more often the hand to hand nature of the fighting allowed of miraculous escapes which were worth telegraphing home at eighteen pence the word [. . . .] It was above all things necessary that England at breakfast should be amused and thrilled and inter-ested, whether Gordon lived or died, or half the British Army went to pieces in the sand.
>
> Ibid, p. 21

Henry Newbolt caught the mood of the hour in his

description of the battle of Abu Klea in January 1885 when the Gatling gun seized up, the Dervishes broke into the British square, and Colonel Frederick Burnaby was speared to death:

> The sand of the desert is sodden red, –
>   Red with the wreck of a square that broke; –
> The Gatling's jammed and the Colonel dead,
>   And the regiment blind with dust and smoke.
> The river of death has brimmed his banks,
>   And England's far, and Honour a name,
> But the voice of a schooboy rallies the ranks:
>   'Play up! play up! and play the game!'
>
> Henry Newbolt, 'Vitaï Lampada', ll. 9–16

For J. A. Hobson all such outpourings were a matter of

> hero-worship and sensational glory, adventure and the sporting spirit: current history falsified in coarse glaring colours, for the direct stimulation of the combative instincts.
>
> J. A. Hobson, *Imperialism, A Study* (1902), p. 222

Equally important were the front-line 'war artists' – Frederick Villiers, Melton Prior (the 'screeching billiard ball') and Charles E. Fripp were the most well known – who provided the visual material for, notably, the *Illustrated London News* (*ILN*) and the *Graphic*. Their work was frequently touched up by home-based artists and wood engravers who imposed their own patriotic style ('an artist's victory over many a British defeat'). How Melton Prior's sketch of the battle of Tel-el-Kabir was given a romantic and heroic gloss by Richard Caton Woodville can be seen by comparing the engraving published in the *ILN* on 7 October 1882 with a facsimile of the original published a week later. It was all good propaganda for the imperial cause.

Ironically, it was Caton Woodville who became the best-known war illustrator even though he never attended a campaign. His large-scale oil paintings, 'Up Guards and At

Them!', 'Saving the Guns at Maiwand' and 'All That Was Left of Them' (the very titles give an idea of their content) were regularly exhibited at the Royal Academy, reproduced as engravings, posters and postcards, and frequently adorned classroom walls along with the equally glamourised paintings of Charles Fripp and G. W. Joy. (Joy's portrayal of the martyrdom of Gordon in Khartoum – however far from the truth – reinforced considerably both the image of the Christian hero and the righteousness of the British imperial cause.) But Elizabeth Thompson, Lady Butler, was undoubtedly the doyen of late-Victorian war artists. Her 'Calling of the Roll Call after an Engagement, Crimea', full of pathos and heroism, took the Royal Academy by storm in 1874. She became famous overnight and went on to paint several more spectacular imperial scenes: 'The Remnants of an Army' (1879), 'The Defence of Rorke's Drift' (1880), 'Floreat Etona!' (1882) and 'After the Battle' (1885). Although her popularity declined after 1914, cheap prints and engravings of her work continued to adorn not only schoolrooms but army mess-rooms and middle-class homes, reflecting the confidence and the patriotism of the late Victorian age.

Indeed, the arts in general played an important role in familiarising the public with the empire. Melodramas, aquatic displays, military spectacles and tournaments were all popular throughout the nineteenth century. They tended to concentrate on great patriotic scenes and dramatic events of empire. An analysis of the plays and musical comedies performed on the London stage reveals a similar interest in imperial events, especially the Indian Mutiny, the Abyssinian expedition, the Zulu War (and the subsequent visit of King Cetshwayo), the death of Gordon, and the South African wars. While many ballads and popular songs of the day also contained imperial sentiments, the production of cheap piano sheet music brought the imperial fantasia into the home. In the open air, the newly-popular brass bands thumped out military marches in newly-built bandstands. And, at the pinnacle of the British music scene, Edward Elgar's imperial marches achieved instant success. Such was the response to the first performance of *Pomp and Circumstance March No. 1*, at a Promenade Concert in October

1901, that Sir Henry Wood had to play it three times in order to appease the audience. The music was set to words by A. C. Benson at Edward VII's suggestion. As 'Land of Hope and Glory' it soon earned its now traditional place during the last night of the Proms. Sung with gusto by the imposing 6 foot 2 inches tall contralto Dame Clara Butt dressed as Britannia, with its promise of unlimited expansion,

> Wider still and wider shall thy bounds be set
> God who made thee mighty, make thee mightier yet,

it virtually became a second national anthem.

But it was the music halls, with their cross-class appeal, patriotic tableaux and chauvinistic songs which were most frequently accused of spreading jingoistic sentiments. According to J. A. Hobson, they were

> a more potent educator than the church, the school, the political meeting, or even the press [. . .] appealing by coarse humour or exaggerated pathos to the animal lusts of an audience stimulated by alcohol into appreciative hilarity [. . . .] The art of the music hall is the only 'popular' art of the present day; its words and melodies pass by quick magic from the Empire to the Alhambra over the length and breadth of the land, re-echoed in a thousand provincial halls, clubs, and drinking saloons, until the remotest village is familiar with air and sentiment. By such process of artistic suggestion the fervour of Jingoism has been widely fed [. . . .]
>
> J. A. Hobson, *The Psychology of Jingoism* (1901),
> p. 3

The claim is vastly exaggerated. But no doubt the music halls helped to create the atmosphere in which imperialism flourished. One performer, Leo Dryden, on account of such patriotic songs as 'The Great White Mother', 'India's Reply' and 'The Gallant Gordon Highlanders', was known as 'the Kipling of the Halls'. The Boer War called forth a host of similar songs: 'Sons of the Sea', 'For England's Bit of Bunting', 'The Miner's Dream of Home', 'The Boers Have Got My Daddy' and the perennial 'Soldiers of the Queen'. Kipling contributed 'The Absent-minded Beggar' set by Sir Arthur Sullivan 'to a tune guaranteed to pull teeth out of barrel-organs'. (Issued with a Caton Woodville illustration of an heroic soldier, it raised about £250 000 for the troops and their families.) But the displays of public emotion which accompanied the relief of Mafeking staggered even the leading music hall stars. On the night of 17 May 1900 the London crowd went mad.

The Reaction to Jingoism

I'm not a 'Little Englander' – a 'patriot' am I,
Endowed with all that's good and great – which no
    one can deny;
I'm proud of all my ancestors, and love my native
    land,
And in her great and sacred Cause I'm longing to
    'expand'.

A frog of old, we have been told, for glory felt a
    thirst,
And, trying well his skin to swell, expanded till he
    burst.
A jingo true, no doubt, will view the moral of that
    story,
And say with pride, 'See how he died, expanded in
    his glory.'
Then let us all expand, my boys, by Glory fed and
    nursed;
Expand, expand, in every land, expand until we
    burst!

> Sir Wilfrid Lawson, 'Expansion' (January 1899),
> in *Cartoons in Rhyme and Line* (1905), p. 59

The increasing imperial frenzy at the end of the nineteenth century was subjected not only to the wit of Sir Wilfrid Lawson and the devastating criticisms of J. A. Hobson, it was also criticised by some of the empire's most prominent supporters. W. T. Stead, to Rhodes' and Milner's surprise, castigated 'the more unlovely side of our Imperialism' in articles in his *Review of Reviews* for October and December 1899 and May 1900. Robert Buchanan protested at the growth of a new arrogant, materialist imperialism in his 'The Voice of the Hooligan' (*Contemporary Review*, December 1899). William Watson issued a chilling warning:

> She asked for all things; and dominion such
>   As never man had known,
> The gods first gave; then lightly, touch by touch,
>   O'erthrew her seven-hilled throne.
>
> Imperial Power, that hungerest for the globe,
>   Restrain thy conquering feet,
> Lest the same Fates that spun thy purple robe
>   Should weave thy winding sheet.

Sir William Watson, 'Rome and Another' (1903), ll. 1–8

Perhaps most surprisingly of all, it was the 'Banjo Bard of Empire', Rudyard Kipling, who repeatedly voiced growing feelings of unease about the increasingly bombastic mood of the British public. At the time of Queen Victoria's Diamond Jubilee, he penned an unusually humble admonition to the British people as a *nuzzur-wattu* (averter of the evil eye):

> God of our fathers, known of old,
>   Lord of our far-flung battle-line,
> Beneath whose awful Hand we hold
>   Dominion over palm and pine –
> Lord God of Hosts, be with us yet,
> Lest we forget – lest we forget!
>
> The tumult and the shouting dies;
>   The Captains and the Kings depart:
> Still stands Thine ancient sacrifice,
>   An humble and a contrite heart.
> Lord God of Hosts, be with us yet,
> Lest we forget – lest we forget!
>
> Far-called, our navies melt away;
>   On dune and headland sinks the fire:

Lo, all our pomp of yesterday
    Is one with Nineveh and Tyre!
Judge of the Nations, spare us yet,
Lest we forget – lest we forget!

If, drunk with sight of power, we loose
    Wild tongues that have not Thee in awe,
Such boastings as the Gentiles use,
    Or lesser breeds without the Law –
Lord God of Hosts, be with us yet,
Lest we forget – lest we forget!

For heathen heart that puts her trust
    In reeking tube and iron shard,
All valiant dust that builds on dust,
    And guarding, calls not Thee to guard,
For frantic boast and foolish word –
Thy mercy on Thy People, Lord!

                R. Kipling, 'Recessional' (1897), ll. 1–30

Kipling's description in 'The Flag of his Country' (a story in
Stalky & Co. published in 1899) of an 'impeccable Conservative MP' who lectures the boys on patriotism, as a 'Flop-
shus Cad, an Outrageous Stinker, a Jelly-bellied Flag-
flapper' who 'profaned the most secret places of their souls',
is surely relevant here. After the Boer War, Kipling rounded
on the British people criticising their boastful idleness and
lack of military preparedness:

    And ye vaunted your fathomless power, and ye
        flaunted your iron pride
    Ere – ye fawned on the Younger Nations for the men
        who could shoot and ride!
    Then ye returned to your trinkets; then ye contented
        your souls
    With the flannelled fools at the wicket or the
        muddied oafs at the goals.
    Given to strong delusion, wholly believing a lie,
    Ye saw that the land lay fenceless, and ye let the
        months go by
    Waiting some easy wonder, hoping some saving sign –

Idle – openly idle – in the lee of the forespent Line.
Idle – except for your boasting – and what is your
   boasting worth
If ye grudge a year of service to the lordliest life on
   earth?

R. Kipling, 'The Islanders' (1902), ll. 29–38

John Buchan later put the case for the 'true imperialism' in a nutshell:

> It will be remembered that some little while ago the
> creed which is commonly called Imperialism was
> tossed down into the arena of politics to be wrangled
> over by parties and grossly mauled in the quarrel.
> With the fall of the Government which had sanc-
> tioned such tactics there came one of those waves of
> reaction which now and then break in upon our na-
> tional steadfastness. The name of 'Empire' stank in
> the nostrils of the electorate [. . . .]
>   [. . .] Whether we call the disease 'Jingoism' or
> 'grandeur' or 'self-complacency', its root is the same.
> It means that we regard our empire as a mere pos-
> session, as the vulgar rich regard their bank accounts
> – a matter to boast of, and not an added duty. All the
> braggart glorification we sometimes hear means a
> shallow and frivolous understanding of what empire
> involves. No serious man dare boast of the millions
> of square miles which his people rule, when he re-
> members that each mile has its own problems, and
> that on him and his fellows lies the burden of solu-
> tion.
>   Jingoism, then, is not a crude Imperialism; it is
> Imperialism's stark opposite.

J. Buchan, *A Lodge in the Wilderness* (1906),
pp. 27, 227–8

4 The Imperial Idea

God has endowed the British race with a world-wide Empire, an Empire transcending all imperial systems which the world has known, not for their own aggrandisement but that they may be the executants of His sovereign purpose in the world. The citizens of the Empire should then cultivate a sense of mission to humanity [. . . .] the fear of God, as Froude says, made England great [. . . .] It is, therefore, in the spirit of Mr. Kipling's great Recessional Hymn, and in no other spirit, that the Empire can be consecrated and conserved.

> J. E. C. Welldon, 'The Early Training of Boys into Citizenship', *Essays on Duty and Discipline* (1910), pp. 12–13

The popular imperialism of the late nineteenth century had many unsavoury aspects which long-standing supporters and promoters of empire found extremely distasteful. For them, the imperial mission was an ennobling task, a duty involving obligations and self-sacrifice, which had a morally bracing effect upon both the governors and the governed. It was a task imposed on the British people by Providence. As the Parliamentary Select Committee on Aborigines in 1837 recorded:

The British empire has been signally blessed by Providence; and her eminence, her strength, her wealth, her prosperity, her intellectual, her moral and her religious advantages are so many reasons for peculiar obedience to the laws of Him who guides the destiny of nations. These were given for some higher purpose than commercial prosperity and military renown. 'It is not to be doubted that this country has been invested with wealth and power, with arts and knowledge, with the sway of distant lands, and the mastery of the restless waters, for some great and important purpose in the government of the world. Can we suppose otherwise than that it is our office to carry civilization and humanity, peace and good government, and, above all, the knowledge of the true God, to the uttermost ends of the earth?' He who has made Great Britain what she is, will inquire at our hands how we have employed the influence He has lent to us in our dealings with the untutored and defenceless savage; whether it has been engaged in seizing their lands, warring upon their people, and transplanting unknown disease, and deeper degradation, through the remote regions of the earth; or whether we have, as far as we have been able, informed their ignorance, and invited and afforded them the opportunity of becoming partakers of that civilization, that innocent commerce, that knowledge and that faith with which it has pleased a gracious Providence to bless our country.

'Select Committee on Aborigines, 1836', *Reports from Committees*, Vol. VII (1837), pp. 75–6

By the end of the nineteenth century the imperial idea had assumed all the trappings of a religious faith. Great Britain had a Divine destiny:

To us – to us, and not to others, – a certain definite duty has been assigned. To carry light and civilization into the dark places of the world, to touch the mind of Asia and of Africa with the ethical ideas of Europe; to give to thronging millions, who would otherwise never know peace or security, these first conditions of human advance.

H. W. Wyatt, 'The Ethics of Empire', *Nineteenth Century* (April 1897), p. 529

It was an awesome destiny, full of obligations, responsibility and self-sacrifice:

Take up the White Man's burden –
    Send forth the best ye breed –
Go bind your sons to exile
    To serve your captives' need;
To wait in heavy harness
    On fluttered folk and wild –
Your new-caught, sullen peoples,
    Half devil and half child.

R. Kipling, 'The White Man's Burden' (1899), ll. 1–8

It was a fate Great Britain could not avoid.

> Why are we Imperialists? As well ask the owner
> of an estate why he is a landlord. We have inherited
> Empire and intend to do our duty by the many
> peoples included in it. [...] We are Imperialists
> in response to the compelling influences of our
> destiny. We are not grouped with nations 'vacant
> of our glorious gains'. We are the heirs of the
> ages, with all the great prerogatives and solemn ob-
> ligations which attach to this high privilege. We
> are, and shall be, Imperialists because we cannot help
> it.
>
> J. Lawson Walton, 'Imperialism', *Contemporary
> Review* (March 1899), Vol. 75, pp. 305–10

The Imperial Idea at its Zenith

> How marvellous it all is! Built not by saints and
> angels, but the work of men's hands; cemented with
> men's honest blood and with a world of tears, welded
> by the best brains of centuries past; not without taint
> and reproach incidental to all human work, but con-
> structed on the whole with pure and splendid pur-
> pose. Human and yet not wholly human, for the
> most heedless and the most cynical must see the
> finger of the Divine. Growing as trees grow, while
> others slept; fed by the faults of others as well as by
> the character of our own fathers; and reaching with

the ripple of a resistless tide over tracts and islands and continents until our little Britain woke up to find herself the foster mother of nations and the source of united empires. Do we not hail in this less the energy and fortune of a race than the supreme direction of the Almighty? Shall we not, while we adore the blessing, acknowledge the responsibility? And while we see, far away in the rich horizons, growing generations fulfilling the promise, do we not own with resolution mingled with awe the honourable duty incumbent on ourselves? Shall we then falter and fail? The answer is not doubtful. We will rather pray that strength be given us, adequate and abundant, to shrink from no sacrifice in the fulfilment of our mission that we may transmit their bequest to our children, ay, and please God, to their remote descendants enriched and undefiled, this blessed and splendid dominion.

Lord Rosebery, Inaugural Address as Rector of the University of Glasgow, 16 November 1900, in *Questions of Empire* (1900), p. 37

Belief in the value and virtues of empire was not the prerogative of Conservatives. Under Lord Rosebery's tutelage, a large section of the Liberal party became adherents of empire. It was a Liberal back-bench MP, J. Lawson Walton, who listed the beliefs of the imperialist:

The Imperialist feels a profound pride in the magnificent heritage of empire won by the courage and energies of his ancestry, and bequeathed to him subject to the burden of many sacred trusts. This is his emotion. He is convinced that the discharge of the duties of his great inheritance has an educational influence and a morally bracing effect on the character of the British people, and that the spread of British rule extends to every race brought within its sphere the incalculable benefits of just law, tolerant trade, and considerate government. This is his conviction. He is resolved to accept readily the burden of inherited dominion, with every development and expansion to which the operation of natural and legitimate causes may give rise, and to use the material forces of government to protect the rights and advance the just interests of the subjects of the Queen. This is his determination. He believes that the strength and resources of our race will be equal to the weight of any obligation which the sense of duty of our people may call upon our Government to undertake. This is his creed.

> J. Lawson Walton, 'Imperialism', *Contemporary Review* (March 1899), Vol. 75, p. 306

According to Walton, nature had endowed the British with supreme governing qualities and the British public school system was geared to provide imperial administrators prepared to sacrifice themselves to duty.

In his 'Clifton Chapel', Sir Henry Newbolt set forth the ideals of the future rulers of the British empire:

> To set the cause above renown,
>   To love the game beyond the prize,
> To honour, while you strike him down,
>   The foe that comes with fearless eyes;
> To count the life of battle good,
>   And dear the land that gave you birth,
> And dearer yet the brotherhood
>   That binds the brave of all the earth –
>
> My son, the oath is yours: the end
>   Is His, Who built the world of strife,
> Who gave His children Pain for friend,
>   And Death for surest hope of life.
> To-day and here the fight's begun,
>   Of the great fellowship you're free;
> Henceforth the School and you are one,
>   And what You are, the race shall be.

> Henry Newbolt, 'Clifton Chapel', ll. 9–24

Joseph Chamberlain had no doubts about the future of the British 'race':

> I believe in this race, the greatest governing race the
> world has ever seen; in this Anglo-Saxon race, so
> proud, tenacious, self-confident and determined, this
> race which neither climate nor change can degener-
> ate, which will infallibly be the predominant force of
> future history and universal civilization.

> Joseph Chamberlain, Speech, 11 November 1895,
> *The Times*, 12 November 1895

The British empire was the most beneficent the world had
ever seen. Its purpose was to bring civilization and light to
the dark places of the world.

Conquest was for the benefit of the conquered. Following
Kitchener's victory at Omdurman, donations were raised for
building a Memorial College to General Gordon in Khartoum. Kipling observed:

> Knowing that ye are forfeit by battle and have no
>   right to live,
> He begs for money to bring you learning – and all the
>   English give.
> It is their treasure – it is their pleasure – thus are their
>   hearts inclined:
> For Allah created the English mad – the maddest of
>   all mankind!

> They do not consider the Meaning of Things; they
>   consult not creed nor clan.
> Behold, they clap the slave on the back, and behold,
>   he ariseth a man!
> They terribly carpet the earth with dead, and before
>   their cannon cool,
> They walk unarmed by twos and threes to call the
>   living to school.

> [. . .]

> Go, and carry your shoes in your hand and bow your
>   head on your breast,

For he who did not slay you in sport, he will not
  teach you in jest.

R. Kipling, 'Kitchener's School' (1898),
ll. 7–24, 39–40

The British empire was an empire with a difference: its
power was used for the benefit of the backward peoples:

We have reigned

Augustly; let our part be so sustained
That in far morns, whose voice we shall not hear,
It may be said: 'This Mistress of the sword
And conquering prow, this Empire swoln with spoils,
Yet served the Human Cause, yet strove for Man;
Hers was the purest greatness we record.'

Sir William Watson, 'The Inexorable Law' (1902),
ll. 6–12

And in that hour I saw my work, and, I think, too,
the ideal of our race. If we cannot create a new
heaven, we can create a new earth. 'The wilderness
and the solitary place shall be glad for us: the desert
shall rejoice and blossom as the rose.'

J. Buchan, *A Lodge in the Wilderness* (1906), p. 32

It was an empire of obligation and self-sacrifice.

The Concept of Service

In Empire, we have found not merely the key to
glory and wealth, but the call to duty, and the means
of service to mankind.

Lord Curzon, 'The True Imperialism',
The Nineteenth Century and After (January 1908),
Vol. 63, p. 157

For Lord Curzon, one of the great pro-consuls of empire, the imperial idea called forth all that was best in human nature. In 1906, in a farewell speech as he left India at the end of his viceroyalty, he declared:

> A hundred times in India I have said to myself, 'Oh that to every Englishman in this country, as he ends his work, might be truthfully applied the phrase "Thou hast loved righteousness and hated iniquity"'. No man has, I believe, ever served India faithfully of whom that could not be said. All other triumphs are tinsel and sham. Perhaps there are few of us who make anything but a poor approximation to that ideal. But let it be our ideal all the same. To fight for the right, to abhor the imperfect, the unjust, or the mean, to swerve neither to the right nor to the left, to care nothing for flattery or applause or odium or abuse – it is so easy to have any of them in India – never to let your enthusiasm be soured or your courage grow dim, but to remember that the Almighty has placed your hand on the greatest of His ploughs, in whose furrow the nations of the future are germinating and taking shape, to drive the blade a little forward in your time, and to feel that somewhere among these millions you have left a little justice or happiness or prosperity, a sense of manliness or moral dignity, a spring of patriotism, a dawn of intellectual enlightenment, or a stirring of duty, where it did not before exist – that is enough, that is the Englishman's justification in India. It is good enough for his watchword while he is here, for his epitaph when he is gone. I have worked for no other aim. Let India be my judge.

> Lord Curzon, 16 November 1905, in Sir T. Raleigh,
> *Lord Curzon in India* (1906), pp. 589–90

Kipling, so frequently dismissed as a crude advocate for imperialism, expressed exactly the same concept of duty and moral responsibility:

Fair is our lot – O goodly is our heritage!
(Humble ye, my people, and be fearful in your
    mirth!)
For the Lord our God Most High
  He hath made the deep as dry,
He hath smote for us a pathway to the ends of all the
    Earth!

    R. Kipling, 'A Song of the English' (1893), ll. 1–4

While there is obviously a political and a propagandist element in such stories as 'The Head of the District' (1890) and 'The Enlightenments of Pagett, MP' (1890), Great Britain's main task was to bring peace, order, good government and justice – 'Law, Order, Duty an' Restraint, Obedience, Discipline!' – to the underprivileged peoples of the world:

We were dreamers, dreaming greatly, in the man-
    stifled town;
We yearned beyond the sky-line where the strange
    roads go down.
Came the Whisper, came the Vision, came the Power
    with the Need,
Till the Soul that is not man's soul was lent us to lead.

    R. Kipling, 'The Song of the Dead' (1893), ll. 9–12

It is interesting to note that the Power was not given, merely lent. Kipling was acutely conscious that the empire was not eternal: the British were only agents of progress who would be deprived of their task once they neglected their moral duty. 'The Man who would be King' (1888) indicates what would happen directly the British ceased to be beneficent rulers. 'An humble and a contrite heart' was the mark of the true imperialist.

  This conception of the British as an elect, a people chosen by God to help accomplish His work in the world, was by no means unusual. As one of Kipling's contemporaries chose to put it:

To say that we are the chosen people of God, is to utter a mere figure of speech. So far as we have any knowledge of the matter, we are the chosen people of Chance. Considered as a race, we are quite imperfect; also we are quite superlative. Other races have more defects and fewer merits; other races have deeper depths and lower heights. In the arts (excepting Literature) we are far from being supreme; and our manufactures do not now stand in the front rank always. But as organisers and controllers, we are the greatest people who have yet had being on the face of the known globe. And as makers of gardens from deserts, of cities from swamps, of comfort from misery, of blessings from curses, we are not likely to be surpassed by any race that shall arise hereafter.

> G. F. Monkshood, *Rudyard Kipling, The man and his work – An attempt at appreciation* (1902), p. 276

Kipling embodied these values in a code of conduct called 'The Law'. In 1893, he warned:

> Keep ye the Law – be swift in all obedience –
> Clear the land of evil, drive the road and bridge the ford.
>   Make ye sure to each his own
>   That he reap where he hath sown;
> By the peace among Our peoples let men know we serve the Lord!

> R. Kipling, 'A Song of the English' (1893), ll. 16–20

Even the jungle is not a lawless and chaos-ridden place – in many ways it is more law-abiding than the civilized world. In *The Jungle Books*, Baloo, the teacher of the Law, tells Mowgli:

> 'Listen, Man-cub,' said the Bear, and his voice rumbled like thunder on a hot night. 'I have taught thee all the Law of the Jungle for all the peoples of the Jungle – except the Monkey-Folk who live in the trees. They have no law. They are outcasts.'

> R. Kipling, *The Jungle Book* (1926 edn), p. 51

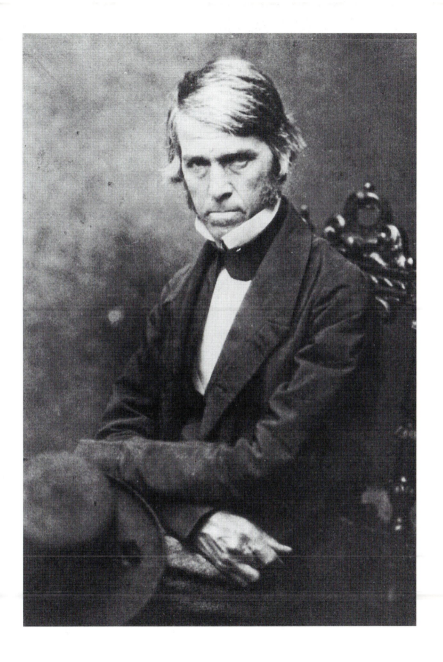

1. Thomas Carlyle, 1854

2. Alfred, Lord Tennyson, 1888

3. G. A. Henty

Men of different trades and sizes
Here you see before your eyeses:
Lanky sword and stumpy pen,
Doing useful things for men;
When the Empire wants a stitch in her
Send for Kipling and for Kitchener.

6. Pillars of the Empire. Kipling and Kitchener,
   drawing by F.Carruthers Gould from
   The Struwwelpeter Alphabet, 1908

7.   Joseph Conrad in 1904

8. E. M. Forster in a Mahratta Turban

This reference to the Bandar-log, vain, idle, completely undisciplined and forever boasting, recalls the 'lesser breeds without the Law' of 'Recessional' (1897) – breeds placed outside the Law not because they are *lesser*, but in not having any Law thereby becoming *lesser*. 'Ye know the Law – ye know the Law. Look well, O Wolves!', cries the old chief, Akela, as they are led astray by the tiger. Soon the wolves are begging Mowgli: 'Lead us again, O man-cub, we be sick of this lawlessness, and we would be the Free People once more'. When Mowgli finally quits the jungle for the civilized world, Baloo and Bagheera counsel him:

> Keep the Law the Man-Pack make –
> For thy blind old Baloo's sake!
> Clean or tainted, hot or stale,
> Hold it as it were the Trail,
> Through the day and through the night,
> Questing neither left not right
>
> [. . .]
>
> Pack or council, hunt or den,
> Cry no truce with Jackal-Men.
> Feed them silence when they say:
> 'Come with us an easy way.'
> Feed them silence when they seek
> Help of thine to hurt the weak.
>
> Make no *bandar's* boast of skill;
> Hold thy peace above the kill.
> Let nor call nor song nor sign
> Turn thee from thy hunting line.

R. Kipling, 'Outsong in the Jungle' (1895), ll. 3–8, 47–56,
The Second Jungle Book (1926 edn), pp. 296–7, 298

It is surely significant that Mowgli, like Kim, enters the service of the British. He has had the perfect training for imperial administration:

> Now this is the Law of the Jungle – as old and as true
> as the sky;

> And the Wolf that shall keep it may prosper, but the
>   Wolf that shall break it must die.
>
> As the creeper that girdles the tree-trunk the Law
>   runneth forward and back –
> For the strength of the Pack is the Wolf, and the
>   strength of the Wolf is the Pack.
>
>   [. . .]
>
> Now these are the Laws of the Jungle, and many and
>   mighty are they;
> But the head and the hoof of the Law and the haunch
>   and the hump is – Obey!
>
>   R. Kipling, 'The Law of the Jungle' (1895),
>   ll. 1–4, 37–8, *The Second Jungle Book* (1926 edn),
>   pp. 29, 32

The Law was central to Kipling's political philosophy and it is equally central to understanding his imperialism.

Kipling was not an advocate of expansion, nor was he a jingo. His empire was a positive force in the world, representing law, order and discipline. It was engaged in eternal combat with the negative forces of darkness, disorder and chaos. The Law sustained the imperial administrators in a hostile environment and from it flowed progress and civilization. Kipling's world was one of work, discipline, duty and service, a world of grandeur, sacrifice and achievement. It was an expression of the imperial idea at its loftiest, freely subscribed to by the great advocates of the day: Rosebery, Chamberlain, Curzon, Milner, Cromer and Balfour. This was the imperial idea at its zenith. To their critics, however, the apparent claim that imperialism was virtually another form of international altruism was sheer cant.

Critics of the Imperial Idea

> [. . .] every Englishman is born with a certain miraculous power that makes him master of the world.

When he wants a thing, he never, tells himself that he wants it. He waits patiently until there comes into his mind, no one knows how, a burning conviction that it is his moral and religious duty to conquer those who have got the thing he wants. Then he becomes irresistible. Like the aristocrat, he does what pleases him and grabs what he covets: like the shopkeeper, he pursues his purpose with the industry and steadfastness that come from strong religious conviction and deep sense of moral responsibility. He is never at a loss for an effective moral attitude. As the great champion of freedom and national independence, he conquers and annexes half the world, and calls it Colonization. When he wants a new market for his adulterated Manchester goods, he sends a missionary to teach the natives the Gospel of peace. The natives kill the missionary: he flies to arms in defence of Christianity; fights for it; conquers for it; and takes the market as a reward from heaven. In defence of his island shores, he puts a chaplain on board his ship; nails a flag with a cross on it to his top-gallant mast; and sails to the ends of the earth, sinking, burning and destroying all who dispute the empire of the seas with him. He boasts that a slave is free the moment his foot touches British soil; and he sells the children of his poor to work under the lash in his factories for sixteen hours a day [. . . .] There is nothing so bad or so good that you will not find Englishmen doing it; but you will never find an Englishman in the wrong. He does everything on principle. He fights you on patriotic principles; he robs you on business principles; he enslaves you on imperial principles; he supports his king on loyal principles and cuts off his king's head on republican principles. His watchword is always Duty; and he never forgets that the nation which lets its duty get on the opposite side to its interest is lost.

George Bernard Shaw, *The Man of Destiny* (1896), pp. 200–1

Even J. A. Hobson, however, did not accuse his countrymen of hypocrisy. In Hobson's eyes, the real problem was that the Englishman really did believe in his country's manifest destiny. He believed the grandiose claims and the high-minded justifications for action undertaken around the globe. A world ruled by the British upper-middle classes would be a far happier place. As Galsworthy noted:

> We always think our standards best for the whole world. It's a capital belief for us. Read the speeches of our public men. Doesn't it strike you as amazing how sure they are of being in the right? It's so charming to benefit yourselves and others at the same time, though, when you come to think of it, one man's meat is another's poison. Look at nature. But in England we never look at nature – there's no necessity. Our national point of view has filled our pockets, that's all that matters.
>
> John Galsworthy, *The Island Pharisee* (1904), p. 167

In 1936, the Indian leader Nehru was irritated by that self-same British faith in their racial destiny and contempt for the views of others:

> the calm assurance of always being in the right [. . .] there was something of the religious temper about this attitude.
>
> Jawaharlal Nehru, *Autobiography* (1936), p. 428

The philosopher, Herbert Spencer, pointed out that claims about exporting the liberal traditions of England were directly rebutted by the methods used by the imperialists: they always depended on the assertion of power. Spencer and the novelist George Gissing both feared that a period of semi-barbarism was about to begin when white savages would overrun the dark savages and the strong nations devour the weaker (see 'Re-barbarization' and 'Barbaric Art' in Spencer's *Facts and Comments*, 1902). Little wonder Sir Henry Curtis, at the end of *Allan Quatermain*, decided to protect the kingdom of Zu-Vendis from external intervention.

In *Heart of Darkness*, Joseph Conrad remarked of imperialism:

> It was just robbery with violence, aggravated murder on a great scale, and men going at it blind – as is very proper for those who tackle a darkness. The conquest of the earth, which mostly means the taking it away from those who have a different complexion or slightly flatter noses than ourselves, is not a pretty thing when you look at it too much. What redeems it is the idea only. An idea at the back of it, not a sentimental pretence but an idea; and an unselfish belief in the idea – something you can set up, bow down before, and offer a sacrifice to [. . . .]
>
> J. Conrad, *Heart of Darkness* (1902), p. 10

While accepting that in the patches painted red on the map some real work was done, the picture Conrad paints of Leopold II's imperialism in the Congo is one of rapaciousness and devastation. The French gunboat firing pointlessly into the interior; the white men struggling with nature to build a railroad and destroying the African labourer in the process; and, finally, as Marlow approaches the heart of darkness, we find the idealistic Kurtz who has scrawled 'Exterminate all the brutes' at the foot of his liberal treatise and joined the devil in his practices. It is a devastating indictment of the Eldorado Exploring Expedition, Leopold II's Congo, and imperialism in general.

As the first decade of the new century wore on, more writers became critical of the empire-builder and the imperial idea. In *Howards End* (1910), E. M. Forster described the 'Imperial type' in unflattering terms:

> Healthy, ever in motion, it hopes to inherit the earth. It breeds as quickly as the yeoman, and as soundly; strong is the temptation to acclaim it as a super-yeoman, who carries his country's virtue overseas. But the Imperialist is not what he thinks or seems.

He is a destroyer. He prepares the way for cosmo-
politanism, and though his ambitions may be ful-
filled, the earth that he inherits will be grey.

E. M. Forster, *Howards End* (1910), p. 342

With the onset of the First World War, imperialism and
patriotism became even less popular with intellectuals.
Wilfrid Owen, viewing nationalistic public school masters
from the gas-filled trenches, declared:

My friend, you would not tell with such high zest
To children ardent for some desperate glory,
The old Lie: Dulce et decorum est
Pro patria mori.

Wilfrid Owen, 'Dulce et decorum est'
(1917), ll. 25–8

'High culture' and 'popular culture' had parted company.

5 The White Man's Burden

It has been well said that a nation, like an individual, must have some task higher than the pursuit of material gain, if it is to escape the benumbing influence of parochialism and to fulfil its higher destiny. If high standards are maintained, the control of subject races must have an effect on national character which is not measurable in terms of material profit and loss. And what is true for the nation is equally true for the individual officers employed. If lower standards are adopted – the arrogant display of power, or the selfish pursuit of profit – the result is equally fatal to the nation and to the individual. Misuse of opportunity carries with it a relentless Nemesis, deteriorating the moral fibre of the individual, and permeating the nation [. . . .]

But if the standard which the white man must set before him when dealing with uncivilized races must be a high one for the sake of his own moral and spiritual balance, it is not less imperative for the sake of the influence which he exercises upon those over whom he is set in authority. The white man's prestige must stand high when a few score are responsible for the control and guidance of millions. His courage must be undoubted, his word and pledge absolutely inviolate, his sincerity transparent.

Sir Frederick Lugard, *The Dual Mandate in British Tropical Africa* (1922), pp. 59–60

According to the imperial frame of mind, the concept of 'the White Man's Burden' was based not on racial arrogance but on the doctrine of trusteeship as laid down in Edmund Burke's famous speech in the House of Commons on Fox's East India Bill subordinating the East India Company to British governmental control:

The rights of *men* – that is to say the natural rights of mankind are indeed sacred things; and if any public measure is proved mischievously to affect them, the objection ought to be fatal to that measure, even if no charter at all could be set up against it. If these natural rights are further affirmed and declared by express covenants, if they are clearly defined and secured against chicane, against power and authority, by written instruments and positive engagements, they are in a still better condition: they partake not only of the sanctity of the object so secured, but of that solemn public faith itself which secures an object of such importance. Indeed this formal recognition by the sovereign power, of an original right in the subject, can never be subverted, but by rooting up the holding radical principles of government, and even of society itself. The charters which we call by distinction *great*, are public instruments of this nature; I mean the charters of King John and King Henry the Third. The things secured by these instruments may, without any deceitful ambiguity, be very fitly called the *chartered rights of men* [...] all political power which is set over men, and [...] all privilege claimed or exercised in exclusion of them, being wholly artificial, and for so much a derogation from the natural equality of mankind at large, ought to be some way or other exercised ultimately for their benefit.

If this is true with regard to every species of political dominion and every description of commercial privilege, none of which can be original, self-derived rights, or grants for the mere private benefit of the holders, then such rights, or privileges, or whatever else you choose to call them, are all in the strictest sense a *trust*; and it is of the very essence of every trust to be rendered *accountable*; and even totally to *cease*, when it substantially varies from the purposes for which alone it could have a lawful existence.

Edmund Burke, 1 December 1783, *Works of the Right Honourable Edmund Burke* (1826), 16 vols, II, pp. 437–8

The belief in empire as a divine trust legitimised intervention, conquest and annexation. It was the duty of a superior civilization to raise others to its own level. The British were peculiarly well-equipped to govern; much of the rest of the world was in need of good government.

Governor-General Lord Wellesley wrote to the Court of Directors of the East India Company:

> We feel that it would not only be impolitic, but highly immoral to suppose that Providence has admitted of the establishment of the British power over the finest provinces of India, with any other view than that of its being conducive to the happiness of the people, as well as to our national advantage.

> S. J. Owen, *A Selection from the Despatches and Other Papers of the Marquis of Wellesley during his Government in India* (1877), p. 687

Macaulay believed:

> To have found a great people sunk in the lowest depths of slavery and superstition, to have so ruled them as to have made them desirous and capable of all the privileges of citizens, would indeed be a title to glory all our own. The sceptre may pass from us [. . . .] Victory may be inconstant to our arms. But there are triumphs which are followed by no reverse. There is an empire exempt from all natural causes of decay. Those triumphs are the pacific triumphs of reason over barbarism; that empire is the imperishable empire of our arts and our morals, our literature and our laws.

> Thomas Babington Macaulay, 'Speech on the Government of India' (1833) in G. M. Young (ed.), *Macaulay: Prose and Poetry* (1970), p. 718

In 'Akbar's Dream', Tennyson envisaged the Mughal emperor welcoming the completion of his work by the British following the collapse of Mughal power:

> I watched my son,
> And those that followed, loosen, stone from stone,
> All my fair work; and from the ruin arose
> The shriek and curse of trampled millions, even
> As in the time before; but while I groaned,
> From out the sunset poured an alien race,
> Who fitted stone to stone again, and Truth,
> Peace, Love and Justice came and dwelt therein,
> Nor in the field without were seen or heard
> Fires of súttee, nor wail of baby-wife,
> Or Indian widow; and in sleep I said
> 'All praise to Alla by whatever hands
> My mission be accomplished!'

Lord Tennyson, 'Akbar's Dream' (1892), ll. 179–89

In *Prester John*, Davie Crawfurd reflects:

I knew then the meaning of the white man's duty. He has to take all risks, recking nothing of his life or his fortunes, and well content to find his reward in the fulfilment of his task. That is the difference between white and black, the gift of responsibility, the power of being in a little way a king; and so long as we know this and practise it, we will rule not in Africa alone but wherever there are dark men who live only for the day and their own bellies.

J. Buchan, *Prester John* (1910), pp. 293–4

It was this exercise of responsibility and the commitment to a task which was worth doing for its own sake that Kipling portrayed in his celebrated poem.

> Take up the White Man's burden –
> The savage wars of peace –
> Fill full the mouth of Famine
> And bid the sickness cease;
> And when your goal is nearest
> The end for others sought,
> Watch Sloth and heathen Folly
> Bring all your hope to nought.

[. . .]

Take up the White Man's burden –
  And reap his old reward:
The blame of those ye better,
  The hate of those ye guard –
The cry of hosts ye humour
  (Ah, slowly!) toward the light: –
'Why brought ye us from bondage,
  Our loved Egyptian night?'

[. . .]

Take up the White Man's burden –
  Have done with childish days –
The lightly proffered laurel,
  The easy, ungrudged praise.
Comes now, to search your manhood
  Through all the thankless years,
Cold-edged with dear-bought wisdom,
  The judgment of your peers!

R. Kipling, 'The White Man's Burden' (1899), ll. 17–24,
33–40, 49–56

Joseph Conrad held a similar concept of service:

> I venture to affirm that the main characteristic of
> the British men spread all over the world, is not the
> spirit of adventure so much as the spirit of service. I
> think that this could be demonstrated from the his-
> tory of great voyages and the general activity of the
> race [. . . .] Yes, there is nothing more futile than an
> adventurer; but nobody can say that the adventurous
> activities of the British race are stamped with the
> futility of a chase after mere emotions.
>
> The successive generations that went out to sea
> from these Isles went out to toil desperately in ad-
> venturous conditions. A man is a worker. If he is not
> that he is nothing.

J. Conrad, 'Well Done' in *Notes on Life and Letters*
(1921), pp. 254–5, 256

Kipling urged his compatriots to labour for the less fortunate peoples of the world:

> Go to your work and be strong, halting not in your
>   ways,
> Baulking the end half-won for an instant dole of praise.
> Stand to your work and be wise – certain of sword
>   and pen,
> Who are neither children nor Gods, but men in a
>   world of men!

> R. Kipling, 'England's Answer' (1896), ll. 27–30

Kipling's ideal was one of self-abnegation and selfless commitment. In Kipling's imaginative world there was no place for self-aggrandisement and the exploitation of the ruled.

The Black Man's Cross

> To be an Englishman was to be born to a great destiny; as warrior and guardian of freedom and justice and peace [. . . .] Of course we heard nothing of the other side of the old Empire: the gold grabbers; the cotton lords of India; and we had no conception, for our masters had none, of a real freedom.

> Joyce Cary, *A House of Children* (1941), p. 34

Imperialism involved relations between peoples. Behind the Kipling ideal, the reality was frequently vastly different. Nowhere was the contrast more stark than in the Congo.

Leopold II's Congo venture was presented to the world as a humanitarian, scientific and free-trading enterprise. In 1876, Leopold asserted:

> The slave trade, which still exists over a large part of the African continent, is a plague spot which every friend of civilization would desire to see disappear. The horror of the traffic, the thousands of victims

massacred each year [. . .] the still greater numbers of perfectly innocent human beings who, brutally, reduced to captivity, are condemned *en masse* to forced labour [. . .] make our epoch blush.

A. Roeykens, *Léopold II et la conférence géographique de Bruxelles, 1876* (1956), pp. 197–9

Yet within two decades not only had a virtual state monopoly in the trade in rubber and ivory been established in what was by then the king's personal dominion, but a system of enforced labour had been introduced whose brutal excesses led to an international outcry and the eventual takeover by the Belgian state in 1908.

More revolting to see without a mask was that falsehood which had been hiding under the words which for ages had spurred men to noble deeds, to self-sacrifice, to heroism. What was appalling was [. . .] that all the traditional ideals of honour, glory, conscience, had been committed to the upholding of a gigantic and atrocious fraud. The falsehood had spread stealthily, had eaten into the very hearts of creeds and convictions that we learn upon our passage between the past and the future. The old order of things had to live or perish with a lie.

J. Conrad and Ford Madox Ford, *The Inheritors: an Extravagant Story* (1901), p. 282

Both Mark Twain (*King Leopold's Soliloquy* [1907]) and Arthur Conan Doyle (*The Crime of the Congo* [1909]) wrote books in support of E. D. Morel's Congo Reform Association. It was Conrad's combination of romance and exposé, *Heart of Darkness*, however, which conveyed the most memorable images: the abandoned railway truck with one wheel off, the man-of-war firing aimlessly into the continent, the dreadful chain-gang, and the appalling Grove of Death:

They were dying slowly – it was very clear. They were not enemies, they were not criminals, they were nothing earthly now, – nothing but black shadows of disease and starvation, lying confusedly in the greenish gloom. Brought from all the recesses of the coast in all the legality of time contracts, lost in uncongenial surroundings, fed on unfamiliar food, they sickened, became inefficient, and were then allowed to crawl away and rest. These moribund shapes were free as air – and nearly as thin. I began to distinguish the gleam of the eyes under the trees. Then, glancing down, I saw a face near my hand. The black bones reclined at full length with one shoulder against the tree, and slowly the eyelids rose and the sunken eyes looked up at me, enormous and vacant, a kind of blind white flicker in the depths of the orbs, which died out slowly.

J. Conrad, Heart of Darkness (1902), pp. 66–7

The final horror was the blackened heads which adorned Kurtz's fence: the outcome of 'unspeakable rites' engaged in by a white man who had regressed into savagery and symbolic of the white man's rape of a continent which Conrad called 'the vilest scramble for loot that ever disfigured the history of human conscience and geographical exploration'.

Perhaps it is significant that Conrad set his story outside the confines of the British empire. British imperialism was never as brutal as that practised by Leopold. Lord Lugard, whilst acknowledging the presence of the same naked self-interest and love of power and profit, argued that the British system was geared to reciprocal benefits:

> Let it be admitted at the outset that European brains, capital, and energy have not been, and never will be, expended in developing the resources of Africa from motives of pure philanthropy; that Europe is in Africa for the mutual benefit of her own industrial classes, and of the native races in their progress to a higher plane; that the benefit can be made reciprocal, and that it is the aim and the desire of civilized administration to fulfil this dual mandate.

Sir Frederick Lugard, The Dual Mandate in British
Tropical Africa (1922), p. 617

Rider Haggard expressed some doubts about these reciprocal benefits:

> Still we may wonder what are the thoughts that pass
> through the mind of some ancient warrior of Chaka's
> or Dingaan's time, as he suns himself on the ground,
> for example, where once stood the royal kraal, Dugu
> za, and watches men and women of the Zulu blood
> passing homeward from the cities and the mines, be
> mused, some of them, with the white man's smuggled
> liquor, grotesque with the white man's cast-off gar
> ments, hiding, perhaps, in their blankets examples of
> the white man's doubtful photographs.
>
> H. Rider Haggard, *Child of Storm* (1913), p. vi

By 1946, even Joyce Cary, one of Lugard's young lieutenants in Nigeria had been forced to conclude:

> Talk of the 'white man's burden' is now a joke. Prob
> ably it is good that it should be a joke, for it was too
> easily used to cover a mean complacence and to
> breed that hypocrisy which of all vices most quickly
> corrupts a nation. But the responsibility of Britain
> towards her dependants was not a joke to the Whigs
> who impeached Hastings; to the men who fought the
> slave trade; to the Church people who have always
> supported the missions; nor to a thousand humble
> officials in the British service whose duty, as they
> were taught, was to the African people.
>
> Joyce Cary, *Britain and West Africa* (1946), p. 48

Even this verdict was far too favourable for a near contemporary who, after five years' service in Burma in the Indian Imperial Police, concluded:

> All I knew was that I was stuck between my hatred
> of the empire I served and my rage against the evil-
> spirited little beasts who tried to make my job im
> possible. With one part of my mind I thought of the

British Raj as an unbreakable tyranny, as something clamped down, *in saecula saeculorum*, upon the will of prostrate peoples; with another part I thought that the greatest joy in the world would be to drive a bayonet into a Buddhist priest's guts. Feelings like these are the normal by-products of imperialism; ask any Anglo-Indian official, if you can catch him off duty.

G. Orwell, 'Shooting an Elephant' (1936), in *The Collected Essays, Journalism and Letters of George Orwell: Vol. 1: An Age Like This, 1920–1940* (1968), edited by S. Orwell & I. Angus, p. 236

It would appear that the civilizing mission did not always have a civilizing effect on either the rulers or the ruled.

The Colonial Administrator

Our life in India, our very work more or less, rests on illusion. I had the illusion, wherever I was, that I was infallible and invulnerable in my dealing with Indians. How else could I have dealt with angry mobs, with cholera-stricken masses, and with processions of religious fanatics? It was not conceit, Heaven knows: it was not the prestige of the British Raj, but it was the illusion which is in the very air of India. They expressed something of the idea when they called us the 'Heaven Born', and the idea is really make believe – mutual make believe. They, the millions, made us believe we had a divine mission. We made them believe they were right. Unconsciously perhaps, I may have had at the back of my mind that there was a British Battalion and a Battery of Artillery at the Cantonment near Ajmere; but I never thought of this, and I do not think that many of the primitive and simple Mers had ever heard of or seen English soldiers. But they saw the head of the Queen-Empress on the rupee, and worshipped it. They had a vague conception of the Raj, which they looked on as a power, omnipotent, all-pervading, benevolent for the most part but capricious, a deity of many shapes and many moods.

Walter Lawrence, *The India We Served* (1929), pp. 42–3

Lord Curzon's private secretary was correct in believing that much of British power in India rested on an illusion: the mystique of the master backed up by possession of the gun. In fact, British rule was largely dependent on the willing co-operation of the ruled. Not untypical was Pandit Bishan Narayan Dhar, President at the 26th Indian National Congress session in 1911:

> We have a government whose justice is exemplary and a civil service which in ability, integrity, zeal, and genuine regard according to its own lights for those entrusted to its care, has no rival in the world. When I think of the dependencies ruled by other European Powers – I thank God that I am a British subject, and feel no hesitation in saying that the Government of India by England [...] is still the greatest gift of Providence to my race; for England is the only country that knows how to govern those who cannot govern themselves.

> Congress Presidential Address, quoted in
> K. Jamiluddin, *The Tropic Sun: Rudyard Kipling and the Raj* (1974), p. 167

Kipling could not have put it better himself.

To Kipling the purposes of imperial rule were simple enough: the administration of justice, the maintenance of law and order, the building of roads, bridges, railways, canals and docks. His heroes were the doers: the district officer, the law-giver and the engineer. These were the men who sacrificed their lives for a noble ideal:

> Year by year England sends out fresh drafts for the first fighting-line, which is officially called the Indian Civil Service. These die, or kill themselves by

overwork, or are worried to death, or broken in health and hope in order that the land may be protected from death and sickness, famine and war, and may eventually become capable of standing alone. It will never stand alone, but the idea is a pretty one, and men are willing to die for it, and yearly the work of pushing and coaxing and scolding and petting the country into good living goes forward. If an advance be made, all credit is given to the native, while the Englishmen stand back and wipe their foreheads. If a failure occurs, the Englishmen step forward and take the blame.

R. Kipling, 'On the City Wall', *Soldiers Three*
(1888), p. 324

This was the experience of the young Harry Johnston in Nyasaland. In 1893, he wrote to Cecil Rhodes:

I have done yeoman service for the British South Africa Company. As far as it was honest to go I have gone in helping them to substantiate their claims, and in the advancement of their interests. I have spared neither the risk of my own life, the abandonment of all ideas of comfort, nor the right to rest at times like other people. I do not recollect having spent one single day as a holiday during the two years and a half which I have worked in Central Africa. Sundays and weekdays, mornings and evenings, I am to be found either slaving at my desk, or tearing about the country on horseback, or trudging 20 miles a day on foot, or sweltering in boats, or being horribly seasick on Lake Nyasa steamers. I have to carry on in my office, myself, a most onerous correspondence in Swahili, which I have to write in the Arabic character, in Portuguese, in French, and in English. I have had to acquire a certain mastery of Hindustani to deal with the Indian troops. I have learnt three native languages besides Swahili in order to talk straight to the people. I have undertaken grave responsibilities, and I have devoted myself to the most wearisome and niggling of tasks. One day I am working out a survey which has to be of scrupulous accuracy, and another day I am doing what a few years ago I never thought I should be called upon to do – undertaking the whole responsibility of directing military operations. I have even had myself taught to fire Maxim guns and seven pounder cannon, I, who detest loud noises and have a horror of explosives.

> Harry Johnston to Cecil Rhodes, 8 October 1893, quoted in R. Oliver, *Sir Harry Johnston and the Scramble for Africa* (1957), pp. 235–6

Somerset Maugham's granite-jawed hero declares:

Year after year I toiled, night and day, and at last I was able to hand over to the commissioner a broad tract of land, rich and fertile. After my death England will forget my faults and the gibes with which she has repaid all my pain, for I have added another fair jewel to her crown. I don't want rewards. I only want the honour of serving this dear land of ours.

> W. S. Maugham, *The Explorer* (1907), p. 208

In the remotest corners of the empire such men are to be found sacrificing their lives 'seven fathom deep in Hell' like Hummil, Lowndes, Mottram and Spurstow in Kipling's 'At the End of the Passage' (1890) or Yardley-Orde on his death-bed, in 'The Head of the District' (1890), giving directions concerning the poor villagers of his district.

These were the men Kipling celebrated, not the men at the administrative centre. Kipling pokes fun at the smart set of Simla society; he lampoons official red tape ('Pig', 1887); he criticises an administrative superstructure that can send wheat to rice-eaters during a famine ('William the Conqueror', 1895) and, at the last moment, destroy months of work by adding two feet to the width of a bridge 'under the impression that bridges were cut out of paper' ('The Bridge Builders', 1893). It is the Viceroy who destroys the life work of Orde by sending a Babu to succeed him; in 'Tods'

Amendment' (1887) disaster is averted by a child who knows more than the rulers of India. Kipling's heroes were the men of action, men of honour and strong character who devoted themselves to their work – men such as the administrators Orde and Adam Strickland and the engineer Findlayson – who represented all that was best in the public school ideal:

> If you can talk with crowds and keep your virtue,
>   Or walk with kings – nor lose the common touch,
> If neither foes nor loving friends can hurt you,
>   If all men count with you, but none too much;
> If you can fill the unforgiving minute
>   With sixty seconds' worth of distance run,
> Yours is the Earth and everything that's in it,
>   And – which is more – you'll be a Man, my son!
>
> R. Kipling 'If –' (1910), ll. 25–32

They were:

> The much-abused public school product *in excelsis*. No parade of brains or force; revelling in under-statement; but they've got guts, those boys, and a fine sense of responsibility. [...] They're no think-ers, but they're born improvisers and administrators. They've just sauntered down the ages, impervious to darts of criticism or hate or jealousy.
>
> Maud Diver, *The Singer Passes: An Indian Tapestry* (1934), p. 243

One literary creation, probably the most famous of fic-tional district commissioners who possessed these qualities, was Sanders of the River. Edgar Wallace wrote nearly 150 short stories based on material gathered during two brief sojourns in Africa when investigating the 'red rubber' atro-cities in the Congo for the *Daily Mail* and acting as a medical orderly in Simonstown. Sanders is said to have been mod-elled on Sir Harry Johnston. Most stories concern some African violation of Sanders' commandments and are full of violent scenes, bloodshed, and improbable events. The tales of Rider Haggard and Henty immediately spring to mind. Sanders' rule is heavily paternalistic, the iron fist not always remaining gloved:

> He governed a people three hundred miles beyond the fringe of civilization. Hesitation to act, delay in awarding punishment, either of these two things would have been mistaken for weakness among a people who had neither power to reason, nor will to excuse, nor any large charity.
>
> Edgar Wallace, *Sanders of the River* (1911), p. 8

Sanders with his superb understanding of Africans, intimate knowledge of the territory he administers and sound common sense, metes out rough justice of an instant variety. He is not above taking a hundred men and a Maxim gun so as to give a public thrashing to an African king. The salutary effect is, naturally, the black man's subsequent devotion which finally ends with the king willingly dying for Sanders. The summary hangings after Sanders has 'crooked his little finger' are equally far-fetched. Nevertheless, for many Britons Sanders remains the archetype of the district commissioner in Africa – despite the very different picture of the colonial administrator conveyed by men far more experienced in the ways of imperial administration: Leonard Woolf, E. M. Forster, Joyce Cary and George Orwell.

The Tarnished Image

> And what sort of people were they? They were ordinary, middle-class people, who came from modest homes in England, sons and daughters of retired government servants and of parsons, doctors and lawyers. The men were empty-headed; such of them as were in the army or had been to universities had acquired a certain polish, but the women were shallow, provincial and genteel.
>
> W. Somerset Maugham (ed.), *A Choice of Kipling's Prose* (1952), p. ix

After the First World War, such writers as Edgar Wallace, A. E. W. Mason, John Buchan and 'Sapper' continued to depict the Bulldog Drummond type of Englishman, the man who acted selflessly in the service of his king, country and empire. The image survived in the popular literature, films and juvenile reading of the inter-war and post-Second World War generations. The intelligentsia and those who were considered to be writers of 'serious' literature, however, had parted company early in the twentieth century. These novelists depicted the colonial administrator and his task in a very different way.

Joseph Conrad had challenged the pretence of benevolent paternalism in his second novel, *An Outcast of the Islands* (1896). Peter Willems and Tom Lingard enjoy absolute power and control over their dependent Malay 'families'. The roles of dominance and submission, of the white man and the coloured man, are laid bare. Willems gratifies his authoritarian desires and revels in the domination of his half-caste wife and her family:

> He was their providence; he kept them singing his praises in the midst of their laziness, of their dirt, of their immense and hopeless squalor: and he was greatly delighted. They wanted much, but he could give them all they wanted without ruining himself. In exchange he had their silent fear, their loquacious love, their noisy veneration. It is a fine thing to be a providence, and to be told so on every day of one's life. It gives one a feeling of enormously remote superiority, and Willems revelled in it. He did not analyze the state of his mind, but probably his greatest delight lay in the unexpressed but intimate conviction that, should he close his hand, all those admiring human beings would starve. His munificence had demoralised them. An easy task [. . . .] This was power. Willems loved it.

> J. Conrad, *An Outcast of the Islands* (1896), p. 4

While Willems exercises his tyranny at a domestic level, the apparently much more admirable and altruistic Lingard, who has made himself 'father' to a whole Malay community, operates on a much grander scale. As the story progresses, the two men are seen to share the same motives and to possess the same faults. The colonial relationship is one of degradation.

In 1919, the year of the Amritsar massacre in India and repressive measures in Egypt, E. M. Forster concluded: 'it seems improbable that a rule which now rests avowedly upon force can endure'. The voice of the callous, authoritarian civil servant and his view of the 'white man's burden' is heard when Ronny Heaslop, the City Magistrate at Chandrapore, declares in an argument with his mother:

> 'We're out here to do justice and keep the peace. Them's my sentiments. India isn't a drawing room.
>
> 'Your sentiments are those of a god,' she said quietly, but it was his manner rather than his sentiments that annoyed her.
> Trying to recover his temper, he said, 'India likes gods.'
> 'And Englishmen like posing as gods.'
> 'There's no point in all this. Here we are, and we're going to stop, and the country's got to put up with us, gods or no gods [. . . .] I am out here to work, mind, to hold this wretched country by force. I'm not a missionary or a Labour Member or a vague sentimental sympathetic literary man. I'm just a servant of the Government [. . . .] We're not pleasant in India, and we don't intend to be pleasant. We've something more important to do.'

> E. M. Forster, *A Passage to India* (1924), Abinger edn 1978, pp. 43–4

Outwardly, Heaslop appears to resemble a true Kipling character, honest, decent and hardworking, but Kipling's optimistic ideals have disappeared and the men of the Indian Civil Service seem, finally, to have 'gone bad' in the tropics.

George Orwell's depiction of the Anglo-Indian official was even less flattering:

> There is a prevalent idea that the men at the 'outposts

of Empire' are at least able and hardworking. It is a delusion. Outside the scientific services – the Forest Department, the Public Works Department and the like – there is no particular need for a British official in India to do his job competently. Few of them work as hard or as intelligently as the postmaster of a provincial town in England. The real work of administration is done mainly by native subordinates; and the real backbone of the despotism is not the officials but the Army. Given the Army, the officials and the businessmen can rub along safely enough even if they are fools. And most of them are fools. A dull, decent people, cherishing and fortifying their dullness behind a quarter of a million bayonets.

> G. Orwell, *Burmese Days* (1934), Penguin edn 1967,
> pp. 65–6

Orwell also demonstrates how the dull coloniser had become a prisoner of his own system. Describing the reaction of a local police officer, when surrounded by a large crowd willing him, for their entertainment, to shoot a valuable working elephant which had previously run amok, he writes:

[...] suddenly I realized that I should have to shoot the elephant after all. The people expected it of me and I had got to do it [....] And it was at this moment, as I stood there with the rifle in my hands, that I first grasped the hollowness, the futility of the white man's dominion in the East. Here was I, the white man with his gun standing in front of the unarmed native crowd – seemingly the leading actor of the piece; but in reality I was only an absurd puppet pushed to and fro by the will of those yellow faces behind me. I perceived in this moment that when the white man turns tyrant it is his own freedom that he destroys. He becomes a sort of hollow, posing dummy, the conventionalised figure of a sahib. For it is the condition of his rule that he should spend his life in trying to impress the 'natives', and so in every crisis he has got to do what the 'natives' expect of him. He wears a mask, and his face grows to fit it.

> G. Orwell, 'Shooting an Elephant', in *Shooting an Elephant and Other Essays* (1950), pp. 6–7

Orwell detested his days in the Imperial Police:

I was in the Indian Police five years, and by the end of that time I hated the imperialism I was serving with a bitterness which I probably cannot make clear [. . .] it is not possible to be part of such a system without recognizing it as an unjustifiable tyranny.

> G. Orwell, *The Road to Wigan Pier* (1937), Penguin edn 1962, p. 126

In a revealing autobiographical passage he states:

All over India there are Englishmen who secretly loathe the system of which they are part; and just occasionally, when they are quite certain of being in the right company, their hidden bitterness overflows. I remember a night I spent on the train with a man in the Educational Service, a stranger to myself whose name I never discovered. It was too hot to sleep and we spent the night in talking. Half an hour's cautious questioning decided each of us that the other was 'safe'; and then for hours, while the train jolted slowly through the pitch-black night, sitting up in our bunks with bottles of beer handy, we damned the British Empire – damned it from the inside, intelligently and intimately. It did us both good. But we had been speaking forbidden things, and in the haggard morning light, when the train crawled into Mandalay, we parted as guiltily as any adulterous couple.

> Ibid, p. 127

Forster concluded:

> The decent Anglo-Indian of today realises that the
> great blunder of the past is neither political nor econ-
> omic nor educational, but social; that he was associ-
> ated with a system that supported rudeness in
> railway carriages, and is paying the penalty [...]
> never in history did ill-breeding contribute so much
> towards the dissolution of an Empire.

> E. M. Forster, 'Reflections in India – Too Late?', *The
> Nation and the Athenaeum* (21 January 1922), Vol. 30,
> pp. 614–15

In Forster's view, British racial arrogance constituted
the gigantic flaw in the 'White Man's Burden'. But to say
that one touch of true regret from the heart would have
made the colonial administrator a different man, and the
British empire a different institution (*A Passage to India*,
p. 51), is surely too shallow and sentimental a verdict. The
Liberal politician and journalist C. F. G. Masterman when
surveying the institutions surrounding the London sub-
urb of Tooting – workhouse, prison, fever hospital, lu-
natic asylum, and cemetery – came to a much harsher
conclusion:

> From the turnip fields of Tooting I apprehended the
> British Empire and something of its meaning; why
> we always conquered and never assimilated our con-
> quests; why we were so just and so unloved. Amidst
> alien races we have brought rest and security, order
> out of chaos, equality of justice, a patient service of
> rectitude which is one of the wonders of the world.
> Yet there is not one amongst these alien peoples who
> would lift a finger to ensure the perpetuation of our
> rule, or shed a tear over its destruction. For the spirit
> of that Empire – clean, efficient, austere, intolerably
> just – is the spirit which has banished to these forgot-
> ten barrack-prisons and behind high walls the help-
> less young and the helpless old, the maimed, the
> restless, and the dead.

> C. F. G. Masterman, *In Peril of Change* (1905)

It was the very machine of empire, involving human denigration and denial of freedom, which really undermined the imperial ideal. To this extent, Forster was right in believing that defective race relations played an important part in ensuring that the days of the British empire were numbered.

6 A Question of Race?

Is it what you call civilization that makes England flourish? Is it the universal development of the faculties of man that has rendered an island, almost unknown to the ancients, the arbiter of the world? Clearly not. It is her inhabitants that have done this; it is an affair of race. A Saxon race, protected by an insular position, has stamped its diligent and methodic character on the century. [. . .] All is race; there is no other truth.

B. Disraeli, *Tancred* (1847), pp. 148–9

Race is everything: literature, science, art – in a word civilization depends on it.

R. Knox, *The Races of Men: A Fragment* (1850), p. 90

The Victorians, despite their love of classification and passion for hierarchies, never used the term 'race' in any precise sense. They usually referred to 'race' and 'races' when attempting to define the characteristics of an individual people, or when explaining differences or antagonisms between human groups. The attributes of the British race and British civilization were almost always confused. Little attempt was made to differentiate between the *biological* factor in group difference and the *cultural* element (ethnicity). Thus the crucial distinction between racial and ethnic (and racial and national) qualities – that those belonging to race are held to be innate and hereditary and therefore unchangeable by education or other social influences, while ethnocentric attitudes allow for the changing and even assimilation of 'inferiors' by 'superiors' in a way that racist attitudes do not – was blurred.

In the mid-nineteenth century, early Victorian *ethnocentrism* (belief in their own cultural superiority) intensified into *racism* (a rationalised pseudo-scientific belief that men and women could be divided into higher and lower biological stocks possessing specific cultural attributes). Acceptance of such ideas made the vague term 'race' a potent force in late-nineteenth-century arguments concerning empire. It provided both a rationale for the government and coercion of native peoples and a reassurance that the superior Anglo-Saxon race, in the humane mission to bring the benefits of British civilization to the colonised, would use its power paternalistically and wisely. In this way, 'race' became a valuable adjunct to Victorian expansion overseas. As Lord Milner stated:

> I am a British (indeed primarily an English) Nationalist. If I am also an Imperialist, it is because the destiny of the English race [. . .] has been to strike fresh roots in distant parts of the world. My patriotism knows no geographical but only racial limits. I am an Imperialist and not a Little Englander because I am a British race patriot.
>
> Lord Milner's 'Credo', published posthumously in
> *The Times*, 27 July 1925

The justification for British rule was obvious: other races were inferior.

> The white man must rule, because he is elevated by many, many steps above the black man; steps which it will take the latter centuries to climb, and which it is quite possible that the vast bulk of the black population may never be able to climb at all.
>
> Lord Milner, Address to the Municipal Congress,
> Johannesburg, 18 May 1903, quoted in C. Headlam
> (ed.), *The Milner Papers: South Africa. Vol. II:
> 1899–1905* (1933), p. 467

It was the duty of the superior race to lead inferior races (the black, brown and coloured peoples of the world), out of the darkness of savagery towards the light of civilization. To put it simply, 'white' was equated with light, goodness, and civilization, 'black' with darkness, evil, and savagery. By the end of the nineteenth century, the visible distinctions of race were being used to justify the extremely unequal distribution of power and wealth in the world.

As British racial attitudes hardened, the 'noble savage' of the eighteenth century, at first usually portrayed as an innocent yet wayward child worthy of change, became increasingly the murderous brute incapable of alteration. This development was partly caused by the changing needs of society. In the days of plantation slavery, Christian slaveowners used Biblical myths, such as the expulsion of Adam and Eve from the Garden of Eden or the curse of Noah, to explain the inferiority of black peoples and to justify the perpetuation of slavery. In the 1830s, when economic conditions altered, the reforming enthusiasms and the utopian visions of the abolitionists temporarily held sway. The events of the Indian Mutiny and the Jamaican Rising of 1865, however, cast renewed doubt on the ability of the 'lower races' to tread the path of civilization. Primitive anthropology, skin spectrometry, craniology, linguistics, and eugenics became the tools of renewed racial prejudice. In the late nineteenth century, when it became even more important to justify the hugely expanded empire and the British right to rule (especially when so many subject peoples seemed to be on the point of extinction), Victorian supremacists manipulated the scientific theory of evolution, using Herbert Spencer's 'survival of the fittest' to demonstrate the inferiority of other races. That the British race was superior, and other races were inferior not only materially but culturally and morally, became a popular fallacy much trumpeted in the penny press.

But this is only part of the story. Stereotypes of other races existed long before the late nineteenth century. The image of the black man was well established by 1850, well before social Darwinism captured the popular imagination. Witness Carlyle's description of Quashee: West Indian blacks,

> Sitting yonder with their beautiful muzzles up to the ears in pumpkins [. . .] while the sugar crops rot

round them uncut, because labour cannot be hired, so cheap are the pumpkins.

> T. Carlyle, 'Occasional Discourse on the Nigger Question', *Fraser's Magazine* (December, 1849), in *Critical & Miscellaneous Essays: Collected and Republished* (1872), Vol. 7, p. 81

Emancipation had turned the West Indies into a black Ireland, a country of idle blacks, each with a

> rum-bottle in his hand, no breeches on his body, pumpkin at discretion, and the fruitfulest region of the earth going back to jungle round him.

> Ibid, p. 86

This was echoed by Anthony Trollope:

> But my friend and brother over there, my skin-polished, shining oil-fat negro, is a richer man than I. He lies under his mango-tree, and eats the luscious fruit in the sun; he sends his black urchin up for a breadfruit, and behold the family table is spread. He pierces a cocoa-nut, and lo!, there is his beverage. He lies on the grass surrounded by oranges, bananas, and pine-apples. [. . .] Yes, Sambo has learned to have his own way [. . . .]

> A. Trollope, *The West Indies and the Spanish Main* (1859), p. 92

and by G. A. Henty:

> The natives of Africa are capable of extreme exertion for a time, but their habitual attitude is that of extreme laziness. One week's work in the year suffices to plant a sufficient amount of ground to supply the wants of a family. [. . .] For fifty one weeks in the year the negro simply sits and watches his crops grow. [. . .] To do nothing is their highest joy.

> G. A. Henty, *By Sheer Pluck* (1884), p. 259

In the early twentieth century, the same view is to be found, in even more offensive language, firmly embedded in textbooks:

> The prosperity of the West Indies, once our richest possession, has very largely declined since slavery was abolished in 1833. The population is mainly black [. . .] lazy, vicious, and incapable of any serious improvement, or of work except under compulsion. In such a climate a few bananas will sustain the life of a Negro quite sufficiently; why should he work to get more than this? He is quite happy and quite useless [. . . .]

C. R. L. Fletcher and R. Kipling, *A History of England*
(1911), pp. 239–40

In this manner, successive generations of children acquired their picture of the negro's qualities.

Such enduring images were the product of many factors, not simply of contact overseas or even limited contact between the races at home. Prejudice against immigrants, whether Irish, Jew or Lithuanian, had always existed, alongside xenophobic reactions to foreigners. But Charles Kingsley's exasperated statement in 1866, that the Irish, blacks and the English working man were 'equally unfit for self-government', is particularly revealing. It serves to remind us that Victorian racial prejudices applied to white 'races' as well as black, and that biological determinism, the natural inequality of human beings, was also used to explain the inequalities of social class. While the middle classes believed in advancement for the talented and the industrious in their own ranks, the working classes were held to be trapped in their biologically determined and historically inherited inferior social status. In the words of Mrs Cecil Frances Alexander's famous hymn:

> The rich man in his castle, the poor man at his gate,
> God made them high and lowly and ordered their
>   estate

'All things bright and beautiful' (1849)

In this way, the white savages at home – the uneducated working classes – were equated with black savages overseas. The hierarchy of races mirrored the British class system. Class consciousness, the everyday experience of Victorians, buttressed colour consciousness. In India, the races were even divided into the more admired martial races of the north and the more 'effeminate' races of the south. In this intensely masculine world, as white was to black, civilization was to savagery, West was to East, the upper classes to the working classes, and male to female.

The Decline of 'Rose-pink Sentimentalism'

> No; the gods wish besides pumpkins, that spices and valuable products be grown in their West Indies; thus much they have declared in so making the West Indies:- infinitely more they wish, that manful industrious men occupy their West Indies, not indolent two-legged cattle, however 'happy' over their abundant pumpkins! [. . .] Not a pumpkin, Quashee, not a square yard of soil, till you agree to do the State so many days of service. Annually that soil, will grow you pumpkins; but annually also, without fail, shall you, for the owner thereof, do your appointed days of labour. The State has plenty of waste soil, but the State will religiously give you none of it on other terms. [. . .] The State demands of you such service as will bring these results, this latter result which includes all. Not a Black Ireland, by immigration, and boundless black supply for the demand; not that – may the gods forbid! – but a regulated West Indies, with black working population in adequate numbers. [. . .] You are not 'slaves' now; nor do I wish, if it can be avoided, to see you slaves again: but decidedly you will have to be servants to those that are born *wiser* than you, that are born lords of you; servants to the Whites, if they *are* (as what mortal can doubt they are?) born wiser than you.

> T. Carlyle, 'Occasional Discourse on the Nigger Question', pp. 103, 105–6

Some 16 years after emancipation, Carlyle still regarded the negro as mentally and morally inferior, only fit to be a member of the servant classes. Dickens was even more scathing:

> [. . .] I have not the least belief in the Noble Savage. I consider him a prodigious nuisance, and an enormous superstition. His calling rum fire-water, and me a pale face, wholly fail to reconcile me to him. I don't care what he calls me. I call him a savage, and I call a savage a something highly desirable to be civilized off the face of the earth. [. . .] It is all one to me, whether he sticks a fishbone through his visage, or bits of trees through the lobes of his ears, or birds' feathers in his head; whether he flattens his hair between two boards, or spreads his nose over the breadth of his face, or drags his lower lip down by great weights, or blackens his teeth, or knocks them out, or paints one cheek red and another blue, or tattoos himself, or oils himself, or rubs his body with fat, or crimps it with knives. Yielding to whichsoever of these agreeable eccentricities, he is a savage – cruel, false, thievish, murderous, addicted more or less to grease, entrails and beastly customs; a wild animal with the questionable gift of boasting; a conceited, tiresome, bloodthirsty, monotonous humbug.
>
> C. Dickens, 'The Noble Savage', *Household Words*,
> 11 June 1853, p. 337

Thackeray was equally convinced:

> They are not my men & brethren, these strange people. [. . .] Sambo is not my man & my brother.
>
> G. N. Ray, *Thackeray: The Age of Wisdom* (1958),
> p. 216

Perversely, abolitionist propaganda, the image of the chained, kneeling slave, pleading 'Am I not a man and a brother?', helped to perpetuate the connection of the

Africans and their New World descendants with the condition of slavery.

In fact, the anti-slavery and missionary movements were to a large extent responsible for creating the popular Victorian stereotype of the negro. In an effort to win sympathy and financial support for their cause, missionaries tended to exaggerate the savagery and the sinfulness of the unregenerate native. In 1906, Sunday school teachers were instructed to:

> Contrast the darkness of Africa with the light of civilization in England. Shew how applicable the title 'The Dark Continent' is to Africa, as inhabited by the Negro race, as the 'Great Unknown Land', and as the Country that, more than any other, has been given over to the 'Works of Darkness'.

Church Missionary Society, *Talks on Africa* (1906), p. 2

The degenerate savage, however, was at least capable of redemption:

> The gospel is 'the power of God'. It cannot alter the colour of the Negro's skin; but it can change the blackest heart of Ham's descendants, and make it 'white as snow'. There is no shade of guilt too dark, no accumulation of crime so great, and no enormity of transgression, that it cannot remove. None of the sons and daughters of fallen Adam on that sin-stricken, smitten, and afflicted continent, are too far from heaven, or too near perdition, for the gospel to reach and relieve.

W. Fox, *A Brief History of the Wesleyan Missions on the Coast of Africa* (1851), p. 623

Others, such as Sir Richard Burton, were less certain that the African could be redeemed. Travel writers, in general, tended to sensationalise their accounts of native life and customs, highlighting such occurrences as cannibalism, infanticide and witchcraft. Cruelty was part of everyday life.

The depiction of savages in the popular literature and entertainment of the day conveyed the stereotype of the black to a wider audience.

This stereotype owed as much to the New World as to Africa: to the droll minstrel, the comic figure of Topsy, and the naturally Christian Uncle Tom. Harriet Beecher Stowe's best-selling *Uncle Tom's Cabin* (1852) created a great wave of sympathy for the slave. However, one particular passage in the book, when the slave-owner Augustine St Clare asserted that his slaves were no worse off than factory workers in England, hit a raw nerve:

> Look at the high and the low, all the world over, and it is the same story; the lower classes used up, body, soul, and spirit, for the good of the upper. It is so in England; it is so everywhere; and yet all Christendom stands aghast, with virtuous indignation, because we do the thing in a little different shape from what they do it.
>
> H. B. Stowe, *Uncle Tom's Cabin, or Life Among the Lowly* (1852), p. 232

When the Duchesses of Sutherland and Argyll presented their 'Stafford House Address' to the author on her visit to England in May 1853, calling on American women to work for the abolition of slavery, a host of American newspapers chorused that these aristocratic ladies should attend to their own country's problems first.

It was an argument familiar to the opponents of 'nigger-philanthropy', frequently used by Carlyle, Kingsley, and even General Booth, the founder of the Salvation Army. Exeter Hall's philanthropy, like that of Mrs Jellyby, seemed to be only for export. One radical newspaper commented pointedly:

> The truth is that the workers in factories are as much slaves to the money-power as the negroes in the United States are to the lash and the law; and yet there is an abundance of sympathy expended upon the latter, while little enough is bestowed from the

same quarter upon the former. When we contemplate the horrors of our factory system, we experience the deepest disgust for the conduct of the Duchess of SUTHERLAND and the rose-water clique at Stafford House, in sending their maudlin sympathies travelling so many miles across the Atlantic, while they exhibit not the slightest evidence of compassion for the slaves whom the money-power rules with a rod of iron in their own native land.

Reynolds's Newspaper, 10 April 1853, p. 8

The position of the working classes at home was akin to that of the slaves in the South.

As class distinctions became more rigid in the mid-nineteenth century, racial attitudes correspondingly hardened:

The English poor man or child is expected always to remember the condition in which God has placed him, exactly as the negro is expected to remember the skin which God has given him. The relation in both instances is that of perpetual superior to perpetual inferior, of chief to dependant, and no amount of kindness or goodness is suffered to alter this relation.

Saturday Review, XVII, 16 January 1864, p. 72

By the 1860s, earlier philanthropic hopes of civilizing inferior races were thought to have been misguided. Only the continuing paternalistic government of the English could lead to *limited* improvement. It was not simply the failure of the West Indian to improve his status both economically and morally following the abolition of slavery, or the continuing equation of blacks with the servile status of labour, or even the on-going wars with subject peoples around the globe which resulted in the imposition of greater political and military control, that led to this conclusion. It was the stresses and strains within English society, including relations with the Irish, which altered perceptions of race relations.

It is true, the alleged atrocities of the Indian Mutiny horrified observers at home. The Whig historian, Macaulay, wrote in his diary:

The cruelties of the sepoys have inflamed the nation
to a degree unprecedented within my memory. Peace
Societies, and Aborigines Protection Societies, and
Societies for the Reformation of Criminals are
silenced. There is one terrible cry to revenge. [...]
The almost universal feeling is that not a single sepoy
within the walls of Delhi should be spared, and I own
that is a feeling with which I cannot help sympathis-
ing.

T. B. Macaulay, *Diary*, June 1857, quoted in
Sir G. O. Trevelyan, *Life and Letters of Macaulay*
(1890), p. 655

Charles Dickens (with Wilkie Collins) recorded similar sentiments in his story 'The Perils of Certain English Prisoners'
in *Household Words*, Christmas 1857. But the activities of
the servile classes at home were of more pressing concern.
High unemployment, high food prices, the financial collapse
of banking houses, a severe winter, a cholera epidemic, and
the breakdown of the relief system, created dangerous conditions for the maintenance of law and order. The prospect
of violence and looting by the 'submerged and dangerous
masses' also complicated the political issue, the pressure for
electoral reform, culminating in riots in Hyde Park. The
upper and middle classes closed ranks as they regarded the
residuum, members of a different and inferior race, and
agreed on the need for more authority in human affairs at
home and abroad.

As respectable mid-Victorians sought to safeguard their
position in the newly emerging urban aristocracy, they became more exclusive in outlook. In their search for gentility
and status, the professional and educated classes began to
regard themselves as a civilized élite in a largely barbarian
England in a mainly barbarian world. Since a black skin was
the mark of servile status, of a savage and slave past, no
black, whatever his background, could possibly be regarded
as a gentleman. And so, the experience of class relations at
home changed perceptions of race relations abroad, as English gentlemen began to pride themselves on their member-
ship of a superior Anglo-Saxon race. Such changes in social

attitudes underlay the transition from the ethnocentrism of
the early Victorians to the racism of late-Victorian England.

The Eyre Controversy

> At times Quashi-Bungo from Scripture refrains,
> And chops up white people, and scoops out their
>   brains;
> Uprises at once the philanthropist squall,
> 'Of course you provoked him', says Exeter Hall.

Punch, 10 February 1866, p. 62

Nowhere were the stresses and strains in metropolitan society,
and the relationship between race and class, so clearly revealed
as in the heated controversy which dominated colonial discussions during the second half of the 1860s. On 11 October 1865,
some 400 creole malcontents clashed with local volunteers in
front of the court-house in Morant Bay, Jamaica, killing several
people. Sporadic fighting ensued. In all, the rebels killed 18
men and wounded a further 35. Retribution was swift. During
the 'pacification' of the island, 439 people were killed or
hanged, 354 after court martial sentences (many were shot
without trial). Several hundred more were flogged, the cat-o'-
nine-tails with wire twisted round the cords of the whip being
used even on women charged with stealing. Over one thousand
homes were burned. The most notorious incident was the
arrest in Kingston of a popular negro leader, G. W. Gordon, a
Baptist minister, magistrate, avowed constitutionalist, and ambitious politician. Quite illegally, he was removed to an area
where martial law had been declared, placed before a court
martial, and the death penalty imposed. The governor later
vigorously defended his actions, stating 'the whole outrage
could only be paralleled by the atrocities of the Indian Mutiny'. A royal commission subsequently praised Eyre for containing the disturbances, but condemned the illegal trial and
execution of Gordon, criticised the unnecessary bloodshed,
and declared the floggings to be 'positively barbarous'. The
Colonial Office retired the governor from active service without a pension.

These events caused considerable excitement in Great Britain. *The Times* declared:

> Though a flea-bite compared with the Indian Mutiny, it touches our pride more and is more in the nature of a disappointment. [...] Jamaica is our pet institution and its inhabitants our spoilt children. [...] It seemed to be proved in Jamaica that the Negro could become fit for self-government. [...] Alas for grand triumphs of humanity, and the improvement of races, and the removal of primeval curses, and the expenditure of twenty millions sterling, Jamaica herself gainsays the fact and belies herself, as we see to-day. It is that which vexes us more than even the Sepoy revolt.
>
> *The Times*, 18 November 1865, p. 8

Large meetings were held up and down the country. A group of dissatisfied philanthropists and radical politicians formed the Jamaica Committee to initiate legal proceedings against Eyre for the murder of Gordon; a group of sympathisers formed the Governor Eyre Defence and Aid Committee in support of the ex-governor. The whole sorry business dragged on until Eyre was finally acquitted of all charges in 1869–70.

The Eyre controversy coincided with the agitation for parliamentary reform in England and for home rule in Ireland. After the huge demonstration in Hyde Park on 23 July 1866, when the police and military were unable to clear the park for three days, further large-scale meetings were held in the provinces, and another great demonstration in Hyde Park was planned which the government threatened to suppress by force. In Ireland, habeas corpus was suspended following Fenian outrages. Thus, in opposing the use of martial law in Jamaica, the Jamaica Committee also had their eyes on affairs much nearer home. The leader of the anti-Eyre campaign, John Stuart Mill, wrote:

> There was much more at stake than only justice to the negroes, imperative as was that consideration. The question was, whether the British dependencies, and

eventually, perhaps, Great Britain itself, were to be under the government of law or of military licence.

J. S. Mill, *Autobiography* (1908), pp. 169–70

The defenders of Eyre concentrated on two things: the necessity of upholding imperial power, believing that negroes could not be equated with European peasants let alone Englishmen; and the necessity of controlling the working classes of England and the colonies. What was at issue was the role of authority and the rule of law in the face of violent social turmoil.

The natural leader of the pro-Eyre faction, Thomas Carlyle, not unexpectedly refused to 'sentimentalize over a pack of black brutes' and the hanging of 'one incendiary mulatto'. Behind him were arrayed the leading men of letters of the day, including Tennyson, Dickens, Henry and Charles Kingsley, and John Ruskin, along with the geologist Roderick Murchison, the botanist Joseph Hooker, and the physicist John Tyndall. The *Spectator* noted:

> the literary aristocracy of England are contracting one of the worst vices of aristocracies of all kinds, the entire loss of reverence for inferiors [. . .] those whose character as well as fate lies more or less in your own power, which is one of the deepest principles of Christianity.

Spectator, 15 September 1866, p. 1024

Tyndall would have no truck with such nonsense:

> We do not hold an Englishman and a Jamaica negro to be convertible in terms, nor do we think that the cause of human liberty will be promoted by any attempt to make them so. [. . .] I decline accepting the negro as the equal of the Englishman, nor will I commit myself to the position that a negro insurrection and an English insurrection ought to be treated in the same way.

Tyndall, 'Report of a meeting of the Eyre Defence Committee held at Willis's Rooms', quoted in A. H. Hume, *Life of Edward John Eyre* (1867), Appendix C, pp. 281, 283

For Tyndall, a black rebellion would lead to an assault on white women. The Jamaican authorities were justified in suppressing the rising with a heavy hand in order to save the flower of white womanhood from lustful, savage, black-skinned males. Hooker was in entire agreement:

> the negro in Jamaica [...] is pestilential, I have no hesitation in declaring; [...] he is a dangerous savage at best.

> J. D. Hooker to J. Tyndall, 13 November 1866, quoted in B. Semmel, *The Governor Eyre Controversy* (1962), p. 125

Behind Mill were to be found not only the Buxtons and Stephens of the anti-slavery campaign, but most of the leading natural scientists of the day: Charles Darwin, Thomas Huxley, Herbert Spencer, and Charles Lyell. As Huxley explained:

> I do not presume to speak with authority on a legal question; but, unless I am misinformed, English law does not permit good persons, as such, to strangle bad persons, as such.

> *Pall Mall Gazette*, 30 October 1866

Support also came from John and Jacob Bright, W. E. Forster, Edward Beales, Goldwin Smith, A. V. Dicey, Henry Fawcett, T. H. Green, Thorold Rogers, Frederic Harrison, and the author of *Tom Brown's Schooldays*, Thomas Hughes. Many of these members of the Jamaica Committee had previously been involved with the main pro-Northern emancipation societies during the American Civil War, and were concurrently involved in the struggles for parliamentary reform and Irish home rule. Not surprisingly, these opponents of Eyre saw wider lessons to be learnt:

> This is a question far deeper than sect or colour. It does not concern Baptists, or black men, or merely the character of a public servant. [...] The question

is, whether *legality* is to be co-extensive with the Queen's rule, or whether our vast foreign dominions are to be governed by the irresponsible will of able, absolute, and iron-willed satraps. It is on this ground that it so peculiarly concerns the working classes.

Beehive, 9 December 1865, p. 4

As with the reprisals against Fenians in Ireland:

without a sweeping measure of reform, justice is in abeyance, law a mockery, and judges the mere tools of the ruling classes in any serious contention between Government and the enslaved people; and that nothing hinders the Tories from doing to the working classes in London as Eyre did to the blacks in Jamaica, but the wholesome apprehension on the part of the Tories that it would be perilous to certain coroneted but incapable heads now entrusted with the government of the greatest empire on the face of the earth.

Reynolds's Newspaper, 5 August 1866, p. 4

Henry Vincent, addressing a public meeting in the summer of 1866, declared:

The Tories are the same now as they were thirty years ago, and as they were last year in the Jamaica business. (*Cheers.*) I will, with regard to Jamaica, give you a rule-of-three sum. As the latitude of Jamaica is to the latitude of Hyde Park, so is the fate of George William Gordon to that of John Bright. (*Cheers.*) The battle has yet to be fought [. . .] but I tell the aristocracy this [. . .] if they dare to cross arms with the people in this great struggle, why the measures of radical Reform will tumble in faster than we dared to hope. (*Cheers.*)

Daily Telegraph, 31 July 1866

As Professor E. S. Beesly warned in the London labour newspaper, the *Beehive*:

> when the upper classes see how [...] injustice to
> labour, even in a distant colony, is resented by the
> the working men of England, they will be careful
> how they trifle with similar interests at home.
>
> *Beehive*, 25 November 1865, p. 4

Contemporaries were only too aware of the close connection between attitudes towards race and class. Unable to deal
with the 'mindless rabble' as they had done at Peterloo, at
home the governing classes retreated behind the barrier of
gentility; overseas, they cocooned themselves in their mem-
bership of the superior Anglo-Saxon race.

Darwin, Wallace and Spencer

> The survival of the fittest is a doctrine which holds as
> good in the political and social as in the national
> world. If the British race ceases to be worthy of
> dominion it will cease to rule [...] Britons have ruled
> in the past because they were a virile race, brought up
> to obey, to suffer hardships cheerfully, and to
> struggle victoriously.
>
> Lord Meath, 'Duty and Discipline in the Training of
> Children' in *Essays on Duty and Discipline* (1910), p. 9

It is not merely coincidental, then, that the 1860s witnessed
a burgeoning interest in the effects of biological determinism. The extent to which biological inheritance determined a
group's physical, intellectual and psychological attributes
(and potential development), had a bearing upon not only
the so-called 'Negro Question', but also upon attitudes towards the Irish and the working classes. If it could be scien-
tifically proven that man's place in the natural and social
order was fixed at birth, then social and racial inequalities
were pre-ordained, thus providing justification for differen-
tiating between the respectable working classes and the residuum, and between the short, dark, swarthy Celt and the
lanky, faired-haired, blue-eyed and fair-skinned Anglo-

Saxon. Humans could then be fitted into the 'chain of being' (in which all creatures were related in a series of gradations) according to their inherited racial characteristics.

Notable attempts at the classification of man had been made by Bernier (1684), Linnaeus (1758), and Blumenbach (1781). The lowest races were deemed to be nearest the apes. In 1774, the Jamaican historian, Edward Long, had concluded:

> Ludicrous as the opinion may seem, I do not think that an orang-outang husband would be any dishonour to an Hottentot female
>
> E. Long, *The History of Jamaica* (1774), Vol. 2,
> p. 364

Orang-utans and chimpanzees were still being classified as human in respectable multi-volume works as late as 1831.

In 1841, Thomas Arnold aroused the interest of the English in their racial identity when he claimed, in his inaugural lecture as Regius Professor of Modern History at Oxford, that the racial character of nations explained the rise and fall of civilizations. The modern age was the age of the Germanic race, of which the Anglo-Saxon people were the most advanced. This immediately sparked off a number of speculations concerning race in the writings of Disraeli and Bulwer Lytton. In addition, an Ethnological Society was founded in 1843,

> for the purpose of inquiring into the distinguishing characteristics, physical and moral, of the varieties of Mankind which inhabit, or have inhabited the Earth; and to ascertain the causes of such characteristics.
>
> *Journal of the Ethnological Society of London,*
> I (1848), 3

Founded by members of the Aborigines Protection Society, the outlook of this society was humanitarian and monogenetic, believing in the unity of mankind (all races being descended from Adam and Eve). Their opponents argued for polygenesis, the original creation of separate species, with unequal abilities, incapable of producing fertile hybrid offspring. Craniologists, for example, argued that by examining skull shape and size, differences in intelligence, temperament and character could be deduced. The discovery of varying skull types from the distant past seemed to disprove monogenetic assumptions that skull shape changed as intelligence developed and civilization advanced. Robert Knox, a Scottish anatomist, intent on arguing that race was the crucial determinant in human history, set out a powerful case for polygenesis in *The Races of Men* (1850). Several of his supporters, led by Dr James Hunt, founded the Anthropological Society of London in 1863 to promote his concept of 'scientific racism'.

That the proponents of the new concept failed to make much headway, was not simply because their arguments failed to convince scientific colleagues, failed to accord with new archaeological discoveries, and were in opposition to the obvious results of miscegenation in Africa and the New World, but because the appearance of a new theory of evolution made the attempt to differentiate species meaningless. In his *On the Origin of Species by Means of Natural Selection, or the Preservation of Favoured Races in the Struggle for Life* (1859), Charles Darwin, building on the geological work of Charles Lyell, argued for the very great antiquity of the earth and long periods of slow change in which creatures, possessing by accidental or spontaneous changes advantageous mutations, slowly evolved by a process of natural selection into new species in the competitive struggle for existence:

> It may be said that natural selection is daily and hourly scrutinising, throughout the world, every variation, even the slightest; rejecting that which is bad, preserving and adding up all that is good; silently and insensibly working, whenever and wherever opportunity offers, at the improvement of each organic being in relation to its organic and inorganic conditions of life.
>
> C. Darwin, *Origin of Species* (1859), p. 84

Darwin's co-presenter before the Linnean Society in 1858, A. R. Wallace, was the first to apply natural selection to the history of man. In a paper, 'The Origin of the Human Race and the Antiquity of Man deduced from the Theory of Natural Selection' (1864), Wallace argued that from one original type, via natural selection, different races developed according to regional variations until man mastered his local environment and ceased to change physically. Darwin explored his own theory of sexual selection more fully in *The Descent of Man and Selection in Relation to Sex* (1871). He ended the book by declaring that he would rather be related to a baboon than to

> a savage who delights to torture his enemies, offers up bloody sacrifices without remorse, treats his wives like slaves, knows no decency, and is haunted by the grossest superstitions.

> C. Darwin, *The Descent of Man* (1871), 2nd edn 1874,
> p. 613

He refused, however, to take any further part in arguments concerning which races were stronger, more intelligent, or higher or lower in civilized development.

It was left to others to formulate the concept of 'social Darwinism'. Wallace continued to argue his case. But it was a phrase of Herbert Spencer's which caught the public's imagination:

> It cannot but happen [...] that those will survive whose functions happen to be most nearly in equilibrium with the modified aggregate of external forces. [...] This survival of the fittest implies multiplication of the fittest.

> H. Spencer, *Principles of Biology* (1865), pt. iii, p. 164

Before long, the theory of natural selection was convincingly applied to political society by Walter Bagehot, in a brilliant essay entitled *Physics and Politics* (1872).

The progression of human societies from the most primitive to the highest and most complex form of organisation provided a ready-made scale on which to plot the progress of the races. Since social evolution and racial hierarchy were assumed to go hand in hand, the Anglo-Saxon gentleman with his white skin and inborn qualities which enabled him to rule the world was naturally placed at the top of the ladder. Other races were ranked according to how they measured up to this ideal. Thus social Darwinism injected a scientific and sociological content into mid-Victorian race-thinking, supporting and reinforcing the changes already underway in racial and class attitudes. Evolution and the 'survival of the fittest' were used to justify ever-expanding British rule, continuing race wars, and the virtual extinction of some subject peoples. In 1900, Karl Pearson provided a classic formulation of social Darwinism:

> History shows me one way, and one way only, in which a state of civilization has been produced, namely, the struggle of race with race, and the survival of the physically and mentally fitter race. [. . .] The path of progress is strewn with the wreck of nations; traces are everywhere to be seen on the hecatombs of inferior races, and of victims who found not the narrow way to the greater perfection. Yet these dead people are, in very truth, the stepping stones on which mankind has arisen to the higher intellectual and deeper emotional life of to-day.

> K. Pearson, *National Life from the Standpoint of Science* (1900), pp. 21, 64

One critic was driven to cry in despair: 'O Evolution, what crimes are committed in thy name!'

The Triumph of Social Darwinism

> Close beside it [a beehive shaped African hut] stood a little black creature which resembled a fat and hairless monkey. It might have been a baboon. The astonished gaze and grin with which it greeted me warranted such an assumption, but when it suddenly

turned and bolted through the hole into the beehive, I observed that it had no tail – not even a vestige of such a creation – and then discovered that it was a 'Tottie', or Hottentot boy.

R. M. Ballantyne, *Six Months at the Cape* (1879), p. 42

There is little to chose between Ballantyne's view of the similarity between Hottentots and baboons and Edward Long's suggestion that an orang-utan would be a suitable mate for a Hottentot girl. Social Darwinism reinforced and extended existing stereotypes of other races. It was the popular literature of the day, however, which ensured their widespread acceptance. In *Scouting for Boys* (1908), Baden-Powell instructed his young recruits to notice the faces of people so that they could recognize them. 'Perhaps you can tell the characters of these gentlemen?' (p. 122). There then followed three facial profiles of a negro, a chinless working-class oaf and, in the middle, the features of an intelligent, alert public schoolboy type. The message is clear: bad looks and bad behaviour go together – another connection between race and class.

The commonly-held late Victorian view of blacks was summed up by Henty:

They are just like children. [. . .] They are always either laughing or quarrelling. They are good-natured and passionate, indolent but will work hard for a time; clever up to a certain point, densely stupid beyond. The intelligence of the average negro is about equal to that of a European child of ten years old. [. . .] They are fluent talkers, but their ideas are borrowed. They are absolutely without originality, absolutely without inventive power. Living among white men, their imitative faculties enable them to attain a considerable amount of civilization. Left to their own devices, they retrograde into a state little above their native savagery.

G. A. Henty, *By Sheer Pluck* (1884), p. 118

The attributes of blacks are usually those associated with animals: a superior sense of hearing, sense of smell, agility, strength and stamina. Moreover, a five-ton wagon rolling over the head of an African causes nothing more than a slight headache (Ballantyne, *The Settler and the Savage*, p. 42).

Another imperial adventure novelist, John Buchan, thought an African native was mentally:

> as crude and naïve as a child, with a child's curiosity and ingenuity, and a child's practical inconsequence. Morally, he has none of the traditions of self-discipline and order, which are implicit, though often in a degraded form, in white people. In a word, he cannot be depended upon as an individual save under fairly vigilant restraint; and in the mass he forms an unknown quantity, compared with which a Paris mob is a Quaker meeting. With all his merits, this instability of character and intellectual childishness make him politically far more impossible than even the lowest class of Europeans.

> J. Buchan, *The African Colony* (1903), p. 290

These were Kipling's 'new-caught sullen peoples / Half devil and half child'.

When the dying district officer tells his soldiers:

> 'I speak now true talk, for I am as it were already dead, my children, – for though ye be strong men, ye are children.'
>
> 'And thou art our father and our mother,' broke in Khoda Dad Khan with an oath. 'What shall we do, now there is no one to speak for us, or to teach us to go wisely!'

> R. Kipling, 'The Head of the District', *In Black and White* (1888), edn 1899, pp. 172–3

the children confirm they need and wish to be ruled. When the sepoy rebels, he merely confirms the necessity of rule: children are not rational creatures and must be disciplined for lapses in their behaviour. Thus did the imperial authority justify rule and coercion of subject peoples; thus were the dispossessed trapped and demoralised in the role of perpetual children.

Another intriguing aspect of social Darwinian thought was that inferior races might represent living examples of the ancestors of civilized man in an early stage of evolution (like the people discovered in Conan Doyle's *The Lost World* [1912]). Perhaps civilized man even had hidden within himself elements of his savage past. Such ideas fascinated Rider Haggard: in *King Solomon's Mines*, before the final climax Good longs for a Gatling gun and Quatermain is possessed by 'a savage desire to kill and spare not'. Sir Henry Curtis appears clad in leopard skins like Ignosi, the medieval Viking and the black warrior, the ancient self and the black, uncivilized self. The journey back to previous stages in European civilization is even more explicit in *She*, where a 2000-year-old priestess awaits the arrival of her reincarnated Cambridge-educated lover. Ayesha is social Darwinism incarnate:

> Those who are weak must perish; the earth is to the strong, and the fruits thereof. For every tree that grows a score shall wither, that the strong one may take their share. We run to place and power over the dead bodies of those who fail and fall; ay, we win the food we eat from out the mouths of starving babes. It is the scheme of things.
>
> H. R. Haggard, *She* (1887), p. 215

She is also interested in eugenics: her servants are even specially bred deaf mutes. It is also noticeable that in Haggard's novels, darker skinned peoples are always subservient to lighter skinned peoples. Black heroes and heroines are also usually lighter and more European in appearance. Nada dresses more modestly, perhaps 'because there was truth in the tale of her white blood and the fashion came to her with the blood' (Haggard, *Nada the Lily* [1892], p. 265).

White noble savages always retain their inherited qualities and successfully acquire the necessary native characteristics; the native's hereditary qualities make the acquisition of the characteristics of Western culture more difficult. When Tarzan instinctively bows to the first white woman he meets,

> it is the natural outcropping of many generations of fine breeding, a hereditary instinct of graciousness which a life-time of uncouth savage training and environment could not eradicate.
>
> E. R. Burroughs, *Tarzan of the Apes* (1914), p. 177

Tabu Dick also retained 'the white man's ability to take mental short cuts and to make direct logical conclusions' which the native was said to lack (L. P. Greene, *Tabu Dick* [1935], p. 21). The 'Westernised' Indian or African, however, remains suspended between two cultures because of the overwhelming influence of heredity. Witness the fate of the English-educated Indian prince in A. E. W. Mason's *The Broken Road* (1907) and the pathetic cry, 'How miserable I am, how miserable must I always be', of another Indian prince in Alice Perrin's *The Anglo-Indians* (1912). The educated Bengali is an even more disgusting specimen:

> Obese, gross, abnormally distended with luxurious and sluggish living, [. . .] a *babu* of Bengal, every inch of him, from his dirty red-and-white turban to his well-worn and cracked patent leather shoes. His body was enveloped in a complete suit of emerald silk, much soiled and faded, and girt with a sash of many colours, crimson predominating. His hands, fat, brown, and not over-clean, alternately fluttered apologetically and rubbed one another with a suggestion of extreme urbanity; his lips, thick, sensual, and cruel, mouthed a broken stream of *babu* English.
>
> L. J. Vance, *The Bronze Bell* (1909), p. 16

There is not much room for assimilation in this literature!

Not surprisingly, inter-racial marriage was even more unacceptable. In 'Lispeth', Kipling does not allow the marriage to happen; in 'Without Benefit of Clergy', the happiness is transient as cholera deprives Holden of both his wife and their child. In 'Beyond the Pale' there is harsh punishment for those who transgress the moral code. The thought of an English woman marrying an Indian was physically disgusting:

> But on his return to his native land, behold, gradually he became another man! Customs to which he had been born and bred laid hold of him again [. . .] in private life he apparelled himself in the garb of the average Bengali *babu*: a collarless shirt worn on his bare body, and hanging over a muslin *dhoti*, or loin cloth, that swathed his naked legs. That was all save for brilliantly striped socks and patent leather shoes with elastic sides. His black hair, parted in the middle, shone with highly perfumed grease; his lips were scarlet with the juice of the *pan* leaf [. . .] and his garments exhaled *hookah* smoke [. . . .]
> This was her husband.
>
> E. W. Savi, *The Daughter-in-Law* (1913), p. 25

The moral is clear: a woman like a

> man should, whatever happens, keep to his own caste, race, and breed. Let the White go to the White and the Black to the Black. Then, whatever trouble falls is in the ordinary course of things – neither sudden, alien, nor unexpected.
>
> R. Kipling, 'Beyond the Pale', *Plain Tales from the Hills* (1888), 1981 edn, p. 171

A white person who gets too close to Indians or Africans runs the risk of gradual deterioration.

This, of course, is the theme of Conrad's *Heart of Darkness*. As Chinua Achebe has pointed out, the evil in the story is African: Kurtz's going native. Conrad associates Africans with violence and lust, bestiality, death and darkness. The journey up the Congo is likened to travelling back in time to a savage, child-like and hellish past. Also, Lord Jim's deferring to his race in failing to lead an attack against white piratical invaders and Lingard's immediate deference to the Traverses, members of the English governing class, are all typical facets of the social Darwinian late-Victorian novel. But Conrad, unlike Kipling, is not writing from within the Establishment. He stands at a crossroads. In novel after novel, especially the Malay stories, he challenges the crude dichotomies of racist discourse: the idea that one characteristic can be awarded to a whole people and that there is a hierarchy of races. His Malays are complex and difficult human beings who offer devastating assessments not only of the Europeans who rule them, but of European hypocrisy and ethnocentrism. Babalatchi tells Lingard:

> This is white man's talk [...] I know you. That is how you all talk while you load your guns and sharpen your swords; and when you are ready, then to those who are weak, you say: 'Obey me and be happy, or die!' You are strange you white men. You think it is only your wisdom and your virtue and your happiness that are true.

> J. Conrad, *An Outcast of the Islands* (1896), p. 226

Conrad was aware of an

> accursed feeling made up of disdain, of anger, and of the sense of superior virtue that leaves us deaf, blind, contemptuous and stupid before anything which is not like ourselves.

> Ibid, p. 254

This was the inheritance of social Darwinism. It is the starting point for E. M. Foster's novel, *A Passage to India* (1924), seen by many as constituting a turning point in the literature of imperialism. Forster was the first novelist of any standing to offer a consistent, damning indictment of the ruling race, the ruling class, and the divisions in imperial society. In Forster's eyes, it was the oppression of the subject peoples which heralded the end of empire.

7 'Too Late'

> Lo, soul, sees't thou not God's purpose from the
> first?
> The earth to be spann'd, connected by network,
> The races, neighbors, to marry and be given in
> marriage,
> The oceans to be cross'd, the distant brought near,
> The lands to be welded together.
>
> W. Whitman, 'Passage to India' (1871), 2, ll. 31–5

> I can connect
> Nothing with Nothing.
>
> T. S. Eliot, 'The Waste Land' (1922), ll. 301–2

The India of Kipling's Simla, E. M. Forster's Chandrapore, George Orwell's Kyauktada, and Paul Scott's Pankot is visibly the same. The British inhabitants of these cities seem to stand still while the code of the pukka sahib becomes ever more stifling as the circumstances of the Anglo-Indians deteriorate dramatically. Kipling's administrators are full of work, certain of their role in bringing good government to India. Forster's administrators, created just before and after the First World War, are much less certain about the permanence of British rule. Orwell's characters have even less confidence in the survival of the *raj*. Finally, Scott's Anglo-Indians preside over the winding up of empire, some deciding to stay on.

In 1883, Sir James Fitzjames Stephen, a former high-ranking Indian civil servant, described the Indian administration as:

> an absolute government, founded not on consent, but on conquest. It does not represent the native principles of life or of government, and it can never do so until it represents heathenism and barbarism. It

represents a belligerent civilization, and no anomaly can be so striking or so dangerous, as its administration by men who, being at the head of a Government founded upon conquest, implying at every point the superiority of the conquering race, or their ideas, their institutions, their opinions and their principles, and having no justification for its existence except that superiority, shrink from the open, uncompromising, straightforward assertion of it, seek to apologise for their position, and refuse, from whatever cause, to uphold and support it.

Sir James Fitzjames Stephen, The Times,
1 March 1883, p. 8

As a consequence, the ruling race ruled from on high, remained aloof, deliberately cultivating a social and physical distance from their subjects. Wherever possible they lived separately, building gothic revival churches and railway stations, regency villas and English gardens in sub-tropical surroundings, even creating an English town in the Himalayan foothills. The environment was ignored and its people kept at arms length as much as possible. In the countryside, administrators 'alone' amongst thousands of Indians travelled miles to enjoy European society. In the towns, life centred around the all-white club, where the Anglo-Indians drank and danced, played bridge and tennis, and participated in amateur dramatics. They retained a strong sense of group loyalty, most being the products of the same school system, possessing almost identical attitudes and opinions, lacking in individuality, imagination and sympathy, but intent on service to humanity.

To conform to the pukka sahib's code assumed tremendous importance. The individual had to submit to the group. In *A Passage to India* McBryde tells Fielding that there was no room for personal views:

> The man who doesn't toe the line is lost. [. . .] If you leave the line, you leave a gap in the line.

E. M. Forster, A Passage to India (1924), pp. 162–3

According to Orwell, it was

[. . .] a stifling, stultifying world in which to live. It is
a world in which every word and every thought is
censored. [. . .] Everyone is free in England; we sell
our souls in public and buy them back in private,
among our friends. But even friendship can hardly
exist when every white man is a cog in the wheels of
despotism. Free speech is unthinkable. All other
kinds of freedom are permitted. You are free to be a
drunkard, an idler, a coward, a backbiter, a fornica-
tor; but you are not free to think for yourself. Your
opinion on every subject of any conceivable importance is dictated for you by the pukka sahib's code.

G. Orwell, *Burmese Days* (1934), p. 66

It was this racial arrogance and racial prejudice which led not
only to overbearing and rude behaviour in railway carriages
but to savage acts of repression such as that committed at
Amritsar. Gandhi, spearheading a campaign of non-coopera-
tion, wrote of the need to:

battle with all our might against that in English nature which had made O'Dwyerism and Dyerism
possible in the Punjab.

M. K. Gandhi, 2 February 1921, *The Collected Works
of Mahatma Gandhi* (1966), Vol. XIX, p. 311

He declared:

although we are not at war with the individual Englishman [. . .] we do desire to destroy the system that
has emasculated our country. [. . .] We consider it
inconsistent with our self-respect any longer to
brook the spirit of superiority and dominance which
has systematically ignored and disregarded the sentiments of thirty crores of innocent people of India.

Ibid, p. 310

It was this tragic failure of imperial guardianship which led

Forster to conclude that British imperialism had dug its own grave. By the 1920s, British liberal opinion, especially that of the intelligentsia and left-wing intellectuals, had come to sympathise with the Indian struggle for self-government. No longer could civilization be regarded as a justification for imperialism.

The Passage From India

> As a result of this doctrine of prestige and race superiority, the Europeans in India, however long they lived there, remained strangers in the country. An unbridgeable chasm existed between them and the people, which was true to the very end of British rule in India. [. . .] They lived in two countries, Anglo-India and India, and the two never met. The one governed the other.
>
> K. M. Pannikar, *Asia and Western Dominance: A Survey of the Vasco Da Gama Epoch of Asian History, 1498–1945* (1953), p. 153

While Kipling, writing from within the establishment, celebrated in his work the values and vision of the 'belligerent civilization', Forster belittled European moral and cultural superiority and deliberately set out to refute Kipling's views about India and its peoples.

Kipling's and Forster's administrators share the same values, but Kipling's heroes become Forster's villains. Kipling's heroes have a natural superiority: they are invariably strong, chaste, selfless, persevering and authoritative. They represent the imperial ideal and reflect the assumptions of the age. They are loyal to the group, unreflective, contemptuous of the intellectual, sanctify tradition, and cultivate the necessary hauteur of the governing race. In suppressing all feeling and sympathy, they seem complacent and arrogant. Kipling's few anti-heroes tend to be weak, selfish, reflective and indecisive. In 'Thrown Away' being sensitive and taking things seriously causes the central character to commit suicide. Forster's heroes, on the other hand, are sensitive, tolerant, critical and intelligent. Forster parodies the demigod and caricatures late-Victorian virtues. He treats the soldier and public school product unsympathetically. 'His self-complacency, his censoriousness, his lack of subtlety, all grew vivid beneath a tropic sky' (*A Passage to India*, p. 73). Forster's heroes do not occupy positions of authority in the army or the administration. They value individualism and personal relationships. They are humane spirits in conflict with a rigid system.

Kipling celebrated the public school code of duty, discipline and self-sacrifice, the central features of imperial administration, in such stories as 'At the End of the Passage', 'The Last Relief', 'On the City Wall', and 'William the Conqueror', in which men

> die, or kill themselves by overwork, or are worried to death or broken in health and hope in order that the land may be protected from death and sickness, and famine and war.

> R. Kipling, 'On the City Wall', *Soldiers Three & Other Stories* (1895), 1907 edn, p. 324

The individual is a dispensable part of the group. When death strikes during an epidemic in 'The Last Relief':

> The chain of men parted for an instant at the stroke, but it closed up again, and continued to drag the empire forward, and not one living link of it rang false or was weak.

> R. Kipling, 'The Last Relief', quoted in J. Meyers, *Fiction and the Colonial Experience* (1972), p. 32

While for Kipling there is no room for individuality, Forster considers it a virtue when, in *A Passage to India*, Fielding stands out against the entire British community following Aziz's arrest for sexual harassment. Forster is inclined to believe that India was lost in the public schools of England. They turned out men who

> go forth into a world of whose richness and subtlety they have no conception. [. . .] They go forth into it

> with well developed bodies, fairly well developed
> minds and undeveloped hearts. And it is this un-
> developed heart that is largely responsible for the
> difficulties of Englishmen abroad.

> E. M. Forster, *Abinger Harvest* (1936), pp. 4–5

While Kipling's heroine, the efficient William, tells a suitor
that poetry makes her head ache, Forster maintains that
those who cannot appreciate their own culture will never
appreciate that of others.

The centre of British cultural ethnocentrism was the club:
the

> symbol and centre of British imperialism. [. . .] It had
> normally a curious air of slight depression, but at the
> same time exclusiveness, superiority, isolation. [. . .]
> The atmosphere was terribly masculine and public
> school.

> L. Woolf, *Growing: An Autobiography of the Years,*
> *1904–1911* (1961), p. 135

Orwell described it as

> the spiritual citadel, the real seat of British power,
> the Nirvana for which native officials and million-
> aires pine in vain.

> G. Orwell, *Burmese Days* (1934), p. 17

It is in the club that the British drop the mask of altruism and
reveal their true attitudes. The 'air of the Residency at Lucknow' pervades the Chandrapore club as women and children
gather before the trial of Dr Aziz. Major Callendar makes
everyone uneasy by calling for the sending in of troops and
the clearing of the bazaars. But Dr Aziz is no Nana Sahib.
Nevertheless, unlike the faithful old native officer who
proudly told Kim and the Lama how he served the British
during the Mutiny and deplored the attack on the sahib's
women and children, Aziz tells Fielding that his grandfather

served against the British and that he would proudly do the same. With Orwell, the decline in British fortunes becomes even more apparent: in Kipling's and Forster's day no Indian, servants apart, could enter the club even as a guest; the central action of Orwell's *Burmese Days* revolves round the election of a 'native' member to the club.

Such happenings were enough to split the empire. Mr Turton, the Collector of Revenue, tells Fielding:

> 'I have had twenty-five years' experience of this country' – he paused, and 'twenty-five years' seemed to fill the waiting-room with their staleness and ungenerosity – 'and during those twenty-five years I have never known anything but disaster result when English people and Indians attempt to be intimate socially. Intercourse yes. Courtesy, by all means. Intimacy – never, never.'

> E. M. Forster, *A Passage to India* (1924), p. 155

Kipling had similarly stressed the great gulf between the races, mocking such attempts at friendship as

> the Commissioner's tennis-parties where the English stand on one side and the natives on the other, in order to promote social intercourse throughout the empire.

> R. Kipling, 'On the City Wall', *Soldiers Three & Other Stories* (1895), p. 338

The same scenario is repeated in *A Passage to India* when Adela Quested, newly arrived with Mrs Moore, naïvely requests to meet some Indians.

> 'Wanting to see Indians! How new that sounds!' Another: 'Natives! Why, fancy!' A third, more serious, said, 'Let me explain. Natives don't respect one any the more after meeting one, you see.'
> 'That occurs after so many meetings.'

But the lady, entirely stupid and friendly, continued. 'What I mean is [. . .] I was a nurse in a Native
State. One's only hope was to hold sternly aloof.'
'Even from one's patients?'
'Why the kindest thing one can do to a native is to
let him die,' said Mrs Callendar.
'How if he went to heaven?' asked Mrs Moore,
with a gentle but crooked smile.
'He can go where he likes as long as he doesn't
come near me. They give me the creeps.'
'As a matter of fact I have thought about what
you were saying about heaven, and that is why I am
against missionaries,' said the lady who had been a
nurse. 'I am all for chaplains, but all against missionaries.'

E. M. Forster, *A Passage to India* (1924), pp. 21–2

The Collector, however, was concerned to give Adela a good
time:

Would she like a Bridge Party? He explained to her
what that was – not the game, but a party to bridge
the gulf between East and West; the expression was
his own invention, and amused all who heard it.
'I only want those Indians whom you come across
socially – as your friends.'
'Well, we don't come across them socially', he said,
laughing.
'They're full of all the virtues, but we don't, and it's
now eleven-thirty, and too late to go into the reasons.'

Ibid, p. 22

Not surprisingly, the bridge party is not a success and the
meeting with the uncomprehending Mrs Bhattacharya ex-
poses the cultural differences between Europeans and Indians and the relationship between ruler and ruled. It is but
a prelude to the more disastrous visit to the Marabar Caves.
The British and the Indians find it impossible to connect. As
one of Aziz's friends observes:

'It is impossible here. Aziz! The red-nosed boy has
again insulted me in court. I do not blame him. He
was told that he ought to insult me. Until lately he
was quite a nice boy, but the others have got hold of
him.'
 'Yes, they have no chance here, that is my point.
They come out intending to be gentlemen, and are
told it will not do. Look at Lesley, look at Blakiston,
now it is your red-nosed boy, and Fielding will go
next. [...] I give any Englishman two years, be he
Turton or Burton, it is only the difference of a letter.
And I give any Englishwoman six months. All are
exactly alike.'

Ibid, p. 6

Forster believes this mutual incomprehension and personal
misunderstanding to be at the root of colonial problems:
without friendship between the races the British empire
'rests on sand'.
 Because of his support for Aziz, Fielding is forced to
resign from the club and is ostracised by his own community
– yet he does not retain the friendship of Aziz. The relationship of ruler and ruled, the lack of liberty, personal dignity
and equality, precludes friendship. At the end of the novel,
in an attempt at reconciliation before the final parting, the
two men go on an epic ride on horseback. The outcome is far
different from that of the ride of the British and Afghan
heroes in Kipling's famous poem:

Oh, East is East, and West is West, and never the
 twain shall meet,
Till Earth and Sky stand presently at God's great
 Judgment Seat;
But there is neither East nor West, Border, nor
 Breed, nor Birth,
When two strong men stand face to face, though they
 come from the ends of the earth!

R. Kipling, 'The Ballad of East and West'
(1889), ll. 1–4

Kipling's men become blood brothers united in the Queen's service. Forster's men are forbidden friendship by the empire:

> Aziz grew more excited. He rose in his stirrups and pulled at his horse's head in the hope it would rear. Then he should feel in a battle. He cried: 'Clear out, all you Turtons and Burtons. We wanted to know you ten years back – now it's too late. If we see you and sit on your committees, it's for political reasons, don't you make any mistake.' His horse did rear. 'Clear out, clear out, I say. Why are we put to so much suffering?' [. . .] Aziz in an awful rage danced this way and that, not knowing what to do, and cried: '[. . .] we shall drive every blasted Englishman into the sea, and then' – he rode against him furiously – 'and then', he concluded, half kissing him, 'you and I shall be friends'.
>
> 'Why can't we be friends now?' said the other, holding him affectionately. 'It's what I want. It's what you want.'
>
> But the horses didn't want it, sending up rocks through which riders must pass single-file; the temples, the tank, the jail, the palace, the birds, the carrion, the Guest House, that came into view as they issued from the gap and saw Mau beneath: they didn't want it, they said in their hundred voices, 'No, not yet,' and the sky said, 'No, not there.'
>
> E. M. Forster, *A Passage to India* (1924), pp. 311–12

Journey to the End of Empire

> The truth is that no modern man, in his heart of hearts, believes that it is right to invade a foreign country and hold the population down by force.
>
> G. Orwell, *The Road to Wigan Pier* (1937), p. 126

The echo of the Marabar caves which remained in Adela Quested's head until she finally spoke out at the trial of

'Too Late' 177

Dr Aziz (thus ensuring his acquittal and her own rejection by the British community) reverberated around the empire. In Africa, Joyce Cary's four novels – *Aissa Saved* (1932), *An American Visitor* (1933), *The African Witch* (1936) and *Mister Johnson* (1939) – dealt equally revealingly with relations between British administrators and their West African subjects. In *The African Witch* Cary, who had served in the Nigerian political service as a district magistrate and administrative officer from 1913 to 1920, writes of the confusion of identity and divided personality caused by the attempted creation of black Englishmen and their subsequent rejection by white society. The mission-educated Aladai in his attempts to gain official recognition and enjoy the company of whites receives three painful rejections: first, when he appears in European clothes in the private enclosure reserved for whites at the Rimi races where Mrs Pratt demands that the brute be beaten; secondly, when he arrives uninvited at the Scotch Club, quoting Wordsworth, and the Europeans leave; finally, when he is beaten and knocked into the Niger for having been alone in the bush with a white woman. He emerges thirsting for revenge, an avid and pagan nationalist, rejecting English values and English civilization. *Mister Johnson* charts the self-destruction of the aimable, exuberant, devoted, and enterprising 'clerk in trousers' who eventually begs to be shot by his white master for his misdemeanours. As the President of Zambia, Kenneth Kaunda, later wrote:

> The Western way of life has been so powerful that our own social, cultural and political set-up has been raped by the powerful and greedy Western civilization. [. . .] The result is [. . .] moral destruction.
>
> K. Kaunda, *Zambia Shall Be Free* (1962), p. 114

Orwell attempted to atone for his own actions by writing about the corruption of human relations under the *raj*. He felt a heavy burden of guilt:

> For five years I had been part of an oppressive system and it had left me with a bad conscience.

> Innumerable remembered faces – faces of prisoners
> in the dock, of men waiting in the condemned cells,
> of subordinates I had bullied and aged peasants I had
> snubbed, of servants and coolies I had hit with my
> fist in moments of rage [. . .] haunted me intolerably.
> I was conscious of an immense weight of guilt that I
> had got to expiate.

> G. Orwell, *The Road to Wigan Pier* (1937), p. 129

The British rulers assembled at the Kyauktada Club are a
pretty despicable lot: unpleasant, heartless and racist. The
central character, John Flory, the only one to enjoy a relationship with an Indian, is driven to alcohol, womanising,
and eventually to suicide, by the imperial situation. He bitterly criticises the 'Pox Britannica':

> 'I'm here to make money like everyone else. All I
> object to is the slimy white man's burden humbug.
> The pukka sahib pose. It's so boring. Even those
> bloody fools at the Club might be better company if
> we weren't all of us living a lie the whole time.'
> 'But, my dear friend, what lie are you living?'
> 'Why, of course, the lie that we're here to uplift
> our poor black brothers instead of to rob them. I
> suppose it's a natural enough lie. But it corrupts us,
> it corrupts us in ways you can't imagine.[. . .]'

> G. Orwell, *Burmese Days* (1934), p. 37

Privately, Flory admits to himself:

> You are a creature of the despotism, a pukka sahib,
> tied tighter than a monk or a savage by an unbreak-
> able system of tabus.

> Ibid, p. 66

The incidents related in *Burmese Days* are far nastier than
anything contained in *A Passage to India*. The members of
the club sense the approaching end of the *raj*. Orwell is much

more pessimistic than Forster and the book reflects the total disenchantment with empire felt by many British intellectuals in the 1930s. Paul Scott later wrote, with hindsight, of the British *raj* sailing full steam ahead into the darkness, with no one on the bridge, lights blazing and bands playing:

> It's time we were gone. Every last wise, stupid, cruel, fond, or foolish one of us.
>
> P. Scott, *The Day of the Scorpion* (1968), p. 405

This attitude was not, however, typical of the day. In many ways the literary fraternity – at least those writers normally accepted into the ranks of 'serious literature' – may have been more sensitive to the changing moral climate. But the very fact that it was left-wing intellectuals of upper or upper-middle-class background who adopted a stance critical of empire and imperialism meant that the causes of empire and 'patriotism' became the property of the anti-intellectual political right and of a more popular culture consumed by the middle and working classes. Typical of the views of the extreme right on developments in India were those of Winston Churchill:

> The truth is that Gandhiism and all it stands for will, sooner or later, have to be grappled with and finally crushed. It is no use trying to satisfy a tiger by feeding him with cat's meat. The sooner this is realised the less trouble and misfortune will there be for all concerned.
>
> Above all, it must be made plain that the British nation has no intention of relinquishing its mission in India, or of failing in its duty to the Indian masses, or of parting with its supreme control in any of the essentials of peace, order and good government. We have no intention of casting away the most truly bright and precious jewel in the crown of the King, which more than all our other Dominions and Dependencies constitutes the glory and strength of the British Empire. The loss of India would mark and consummate the downfall of the British Empire.

That organism would pass at a stroke out of life into history. From such a catastrophe there would be no recovery. [. . .]

It is alarming and also nauseating to see Mr Gandhi, a seditious Middle Temple lawyer, now posing as a fakir of a type well-known in the East, striding half-naked up the steps of the Vice-regal palace, while he is still organizing and conducting a defiant campaign of civil disobedience, to parley on equal terms with the representative of the King-Emperor.

W. S. Churchill, 12 March 1931, R. R. James (ed.), *Winston S. Churchill: His Complete Speeches* (1974), Vol. V, pp. 4, 982–6

Churchill's views may have been extreme, but his belief in king, country and empire was not unfashionable in the 1930s. Even Orwell agreed that the popular mass media of the day promoted:

patriotism, religion, the Empire, the family, the sanctity of marriage, the old school tie, birth, breeding, honour and discipline.

G. Orwell, *Collected Essays* (1968), Vol. 1, p. 564

Such values continued to hold centre stage into the 1950s.

As suggested in the opening chapter, in the early twentieth century a great chasm opened up between the views of the intellectual élite and the mass of the people in the country. The popular writers with a mass readership in the inter-war period were Edgar Wallace, Sapper, John Buchan and P. C. Wren. Their heroes tended to be of the Bulldog Drummond variety – public-school educated lovers of country and empire. The public schools, so bitterly castigated by Forster and Orwell were celebrated in James Hilton's *Goodbye Mr. Chips* (1934) and in the pages of the *Magnet* and *Gem*. The imperial epic was also one of the most regular box-office successes in the cinema. *The Four Feathers* (1929), *King of the Khyber Rifles* (1929), *The Lost Patrol* (1934), *Clive of India* (1935), *The Lives of a Bengal Lancer* (1935), *Sanders of the River* (1935), *Rhodes of Africa* (1936), *Under Two Flags* (1936), *The Great Barrier* (1936), *King Solomon's Mines* (1937), *The Drum* (1938), *Gunga Din* (1939), *Stanley and Livingstone* (1939) and, again, *The Four Feathers* (1939), were all in the great imperial adventure tradition. Significantly, this continued into the 1950s – *King Solomon's Mines* (1950), *Kim* (1951), *Soldiers Three* (1951), *Storm over Africa* (1953), *King of the Khyber Rifles* (1954), *Khyber Patrol* (1954), *Storm over the Nile* (1955), *Yangtze Incident* (1957) and *North West Frontier* (1959) – with *Zulu* (1963) and *Khartoum* (1966) still to come. This can be matched in the juvenile literature of the 1930s through to the 1950s. G. A. Henty remained a staple diet. Frank Richards, Percy F. Westerman, and W. E. Johns continued writing their patriotic stories, tinged with xenophobia and racism, in the inter-war years. The *Rover*, *Wizard* and *Hotspur* took over where the *Gem* and *Magnet* left off. Cigarette cards and postcards with an imperial content remained popular. Series of books on missionary and colonial heroes, daring deeds of empire, and traditional-style school textbooks, continued to be produced alongside *The Wonder Book of Empire*, the *New Empire Annual*, *The Empire Annual for Girls* and the *Youth Empire Annuals* of the 1940s and 1950s. Major Ney's Empire Youth Movement continued into the 1960s. Empire Day broadcasts and the royal visits overseas of George V, the future King Edward VIII, George VI, and the young Queen Elizabeth II, continued to arouse public interest. In short, it was not until well into the 1950s that the empire began to lose its grip on many aspects of popular culture.

Amazingly, the same old patriotic attitudes, reverence for royalty, belief in empire, the class system, deference to one's superiors, the old school tie and the old-boy network, as well as Victorian ideas about race, had survived two world wars and the emergence of the two super powers. However, the events of the 1950s – the Suez crisis of 1956, the Hola Camp incident in 1959, and the declaration that Nyasaland was virtually a police state – the winds of change blowing through Africa commented on by Harold Macmillan in a speech to the South African parliament in 1960, and Britain's first attempt to join the Common Market, heralded the final demise of the nineteenth-century world-view. With the

Commonwealth no longer a white man's club, the British government finally followed the intelligentsia in turning its back on the empire.

But reminders of our imperial past abound. Every now and then the British public is swept by a wave of nostalgia for the days of imperial greatness – such as that which accompanied the showing of 'The Jewel in the Crown' (the televised version of Paul Scott's *Raj Quartet*), or the outburst of jingoism during the Falklands crisis. The imperial experience remains an important legacy of the last 200 years of British history. The age of Disraeli, Gladstone, Salisbury, Rosebery and Chamberlain, the era of Kipling, Henty, Haggard, Newbolt and Buchan, witnessed extraordinary events and produced a culture, both high and low, saturated in imperial ideology such as had never been seen before, and presumably will never be seen again. It is not surprising that these years continue to fascinate historians and literary specialists alike.

Chronological Table

Date	Contemporary events	Publications
1834	Abolition of slavery in the British empire	Tennyson, 'O Mother Britain Lift Thou Up'
1837	Accession of Queen Victoria; Canadian Rebellions	McCulloch, *Statistical Account of the British Empire*
1838	Apprenticeship system in the West Indies abolished	Thackeray, *Tremendous Adventures of Major Gahagan*
1839	Lord Durham's Report; Aden annexed; First Afghan War (1839–42)	Carlyle, *Chartism*; Taylor, *Confessions of a Thug*
1840	New Zealand annexed; Union of the two Canadas	Buxton, *The African Slave Trade*; Taylor, *Tippoo Sultaun*
1841	Livingstone in Africa; Buxton's Niger expedition; Retreat from Kabul	Carlyle, *Heroes & Hero Worship*; Marryat, *Masterman Ready*; Merivale, *Lectures on Colonization and Colonies*
1842	Hong Kong annexed	Tennyson, *Poems*
1843	Natal annexed;	Carlyle, *Past & Present*

	Maori Wars (1843–47); Sind conquered	
1845	First Sikh War	Martineau, *Dawn Island*
1846	Kaffraria and Labuan annexed	
1847	Governor of Cape Colony becomes High Commissioner for South Africa	Dickens, *Dombey & Son*; Disraeli, *Tancred*; Longfellow, '*Evangeline*'; Thackeray, *Vanity Fair*
1848	Transvaal and Orange Free State annexed; Second Sikh War; Satara, Jaipur & Sambalpur 'lapse' to the British crown	Ballantyne, *Hudson Bay*; Mill, *Principles of Political Economy*; Thackeray, *History of Pendennis*
1849	Navigation Acts abolished	Carlyle, '*The Nigger Question*'; Dickens, *David Copperfield*; Lytton, *The Caxtons*; Wakefield, *View of the Art of Colonization*
1850	Australian Colonies Government Act; Baghat lapses	Carlyle, *Latter-Day Pamphlets*; Knox, *Races of Men*
1851	Great Exhibition; Australian gold rush; Victoria becomes a separate colony	
1852	Sand River Convention; Lower Burma annexed; Udaipur lapses	Burton, *Mission to Gelele*; Dickens, *Bleak House*; Stowe, *Uncle Tom's Cabin*

1853 Jhansi lapses	Dickens, '*The Noble Savage*'; Thackeray, *The Newcomes*
1854 Bloemfontein Convention; Nagpur lapses; Crimean War (1854–6)	
1855 New constitutions for most Australian colonies	C. Kingsley, *Westward Ho!*
1856 Oudh annexed; Treaty of Paris ends Crimean War	Burton, *First Footsteps in East Africa*; Reade, *It Is Never Too Late to Mend*
1857 May: Indian Mutiny-Rebellion; June: Fall of Cawnpore; Siege of Lucknow and Delhi; Sept: Delhi recaptured; Nov: Lucknow relieved	Ballantyne, *The Coral Island*; Dickens, '*Perils of Certain English Prisoners*'; Livingstone, *Missionary Travels*
1858 Proclamation of British rule over India; Government of India Act; British Columbia established	Ballantyne, *Young Fur Traders*; *Ungava*; Trollope, *The Three Clerks*
1859 Palmerston Prime Minister; Queensland becomes a separate colony	Darwin, *Origin of Species*; H. Kingsley, *Recollections of Geoffrey Hamlyn*; Trollope, *West Indies & the Spanish Main*
1860 Maori Wars resume (to 1870); Kowloon leased	Dickens, *Great Expectations*; Russell, *My Diary in India in the Year 1858–59*

1861	Lagos annexed; Indian Councils Act	Ballantyne, *The Gorilla Hunters*
1862	British representative established at Mandalay	C. Kingsley, *Water Babies*; Trollope, *North America*
1863	Ashanti War (1863–4); Anthropological Society founded	Huxley, *Man's Place in Nature*; Lyell, *The Antiquity of Man*; Smith, *The Empire*
1864	Ionian Islands ceded to Greece	Lawrence, *Maurice Derring*; Spencer, *Principles of Biology*
1865	Select Committee on West African Settlements; Morant Bay (Jamaica) rising	Arnold, 'Heine's Grave'; Bury, *Exodus of the Western Nations*; H. Kingsley, *Hillyers and Burtons*
1867	Abyssinian Expedition; Straits Settlements Colony; Dominion of Canada created	Carlyle, *Shooting Niagra*; Hume, *Life of John Edward Eyre*; Mayne Reid, *Giraffe Hunters*
1868	Basutoland annexed; Colonial Society founded; Dec: Gladstone Prime Minister	Collins, *The Moonstone*; Dilke, *Greater Britain*; Grant, *First Love and Last Love*
1869	Suez Canal opened; Hudson's Bay Company cedes lands to Canadian Dominion	H. Kingsley, *Stretton*; Wallace, *The Malay Archipelago*

1870	Red River Expedition; Manitoba created	Disraeli, *Lothair*; Ruskin, *Inaugural Lecture*
1871	Griqualand West annexed; British Columbia joins Canadian Dominion; Leeward Islands federated	Austin, 'The Golden Age'; Darwin, *The Descent of Man*; Lytton, *The Coming Race*; Whitman, 'Passage to India'
1872	Responsible government in Cape Colony; Disraeli's Crystal Palace speech	Bagehot, *Physics and Politics*; Butler, *Erewhon*; Stanley, *How I Found Livingstone*; Taylor, *Seeta*; Tennyson, 'To the Queen'
1873	Ashanti War (1873–4); Prince Edward Island joins Canadian Dominion	Ballantyne, *Black Ivory*; Trollope, *Australia & New Zealand*
1874	Disraeli Prime Minister; Fiji Islands annexed; Resident system introduced into Western Malay States; Lady Butler's 'Roll Call'	Henty, *The March to Coomassie*
1875	Purchase Suez Canal shares; Carnarvon launches South African confederation scheme	W. Forster, *Our Colonial Empire*; Thomson, *The Straits of Malacca*; Thorburn, *The Great Game*
1876	Victoria proclaimed Empress of India; Bulgarian atrocities	Chesney, *The Dilemma*; Jenkins, *The Blot on the Queen's Head*

1877	Annexation of the Transvaal; Western Pacific High Commission created; G. W. Hunt's, *'By Jingo!'*	Ballantyne, *Settler and Savage*; Dicey, *'Gladstone & our Empire'*; Gladstone, *'Aggression on Egypt'*
1878	Congress of Berlin; Cyprus occupied; 2nd Anglo-Afghan War; Walvis Bay Protectorate	Carnarvon, *'Imperial Administration'*; Gladstone, *'England's Mission'*; Lowe, *'Imperialism'*; Stanley, *Through the Dark Continent*; Tennyson, *'The Revenge'*
1879	Anglo-Zulu War; Third Anglo-Afghan War; Dual Control established in Egypt; Gladstone's Midlothian campaign; *Boy's Own Paper* launched; Butler, *'Remnants of an Army'*	Escott, *Pillars of the Empire*; Gladstone, *Midlothian Speeches*; Tennyson, *'Defence of Lucknow'*; Trollope, *John Caldigate*; Wedderburn, *Modern Imperialism in India*
1880	Gladstone Prime Minister; First Anglo-Boer War (1880–1); Butler, *'Defence of Rorke's Drift'*	Ballantyne, *Red Man's Revenge*; Froude, *Two Lectures on South Africa*
1881	British North Borneo Company chartered; Revolt of the Mahdi in Sudan	Haggard, *Cetewayo & his White Neighbours*; Henty, *In Times of Peril*
1882	British occupation of Egypt; Butler, *'Floreat Etona'*	Tennyson, *'Hands All Round'*

1883	Cromer becomes British Agent and Consul General in Egypt	Schreiner, *Story of an African Farm*; Seeley, *Expansion of England*; Stevenson, *Treasure Island*
1884	Anglo-Portuguese Congo Treaty; British Somaliland Protectorate; Papua annexed; Berlin West Africa Conference	Haggard, *Witch's Head*; Henty, *By Sheer Pluck*; *With Clive in India*; Kingston, *Hendricks the Hunter*
1885	Death of Gordon at Khartoum; Third Anglo-Burmese War; Anglo-Russian Penjdeh crisis; Oil Rivers Protectorate; Bechuanaland Protectorate; Indian National Congress formed; Lady Butler's '*After the Battle*'	Haggard, *King Solomon's Mines*; Henty, *The Young Colonists*; *True to the Old Flag*; Watson, '*Gladstone*'
1886	Salisbury Prime Minister; Gold discovered in Transvaal; Upper Burma annexed; Anglo-German East African agreement; Royal Niger Company chartered; Indian and Colonial Exhibition	Froude, *Oceana*; Henty, *For Name and Fame*; Kipling, *Departmental Ditties*; Tennyson, '*The opening of the Indian and Colonial Exhibition by the Queen*'
1887	Victoria's Golden Jubilee; New Hebrides Condominium; Colonial Conference; Informal Anglo-Russian division of Persia into spheres of interest	Haggard, *She*; *Allan Quatermain*; Henty, *With Wolfe in Canada*; *A Final Reckoning*; Tennyson, '*On the Jubilee of Queen Victoria*'

1888	Imperial British East Africa Company chartered; Protectorates over Sarawak, Brunei, North Borneo and Cook Islands; Zululand annexed	Froude, *The English in the West Indies*; Kipling, *In Black and White*; *Plain Tales from the Hills*; *Soldiers Three*; *Wee Willie Winkie*
1889	British South Africa Company chartered; Salisbury announces decision to remain in Egypt for the forseeable future	Kipling, '*Ballad of East and West*'; Stanley, *My Kalulu*; Wallace, *Darwinism*
1890	Cecil Rhodes Prime Minister of Cape Colony; Anglo-German Heligoland-Zanzibar Treaty; Anglo-French treaty concerning West Africa	Dilke, *Problems of Greater Britain*; Doyle, *Sign of Four*; Kipling, *The Light That Failed*; Stanley, *In Darkest Africa*
1891	Anglo-Portuguese agreement over Central and East Africa; Nyasaland Protectorate	Henley, *Lyra Heroica*; Henty, *Maori and Settler*; Kipling, *Life's Handicap*
1892	Gladstone Prime Minister; Protectorate over Gilbert and Ellice Islands; Indian Councils Act; Imperial Institute founded; *Chums* founded	Haggard, *Nada the Lily*; Henley, '*Pro Rege Nostro*'; Henty, *The Dash for Khartoum*; *Held Fast For England*; Kipling, *Barrack Room Ballards*; Tennyson, '*Akbar's Dream*'
1893	Responsible government in Natal; British South Africa Company war against the Ndebele; *Halfpenny Marvel* founded	Keltie, *Partition of Africa*; Kipling, *Many Inventions*; '*Song of the English*' and '*Song of the Dead*'; Pearson, *National Life and*

		Character; Stevenson, *Beach of Falesá*
1894	Rosebery Prime Minister; Uganda Protectorate; *Pluck* founded; *Union Jack* founded	Henty, *Through the Sikh War*; Kidd, *Social Evolution*; Kipling, *The Jungle Book*; Stevenson, *Ebb-Tide*
1895	Salisbury Prime Minister; Chamberlain Colonial Secretary; Protectorate over Kenya; Dec: Jameson Raid	Conrad, *Almayer's Folly*; Kipling, *The Second Jungle Book*; 'William the Conqueror'
1896	Rhodes resigns as Prime Minister of Cape Colony; Lord Kitchener advances in the Sudan; Fourth Ashanti War; Federation of Malay States (Perak, Selangor, Negri Sembilan, Pahang); Alfred Austin becomes Poet Laureate; *Daily Mail* founded	Austin, 'Jameson's Ride'; Baden-Powell, *Downfall of Prempeh*; Conrad, *An Outcast of the Islands*; Henty, *The Tiger of Mysore*; Kipling, *The Seven Seas*; 'England's Answer'; Shaw, *The Man of Destiny*; Steele, *On the Face of the Waters*; Stevenson, *In the South Seas*
1897	Victoria's Diamond Jubilee; Milner appointed High Commissioner for South Africa; Colonial Conference; Protectorate over the Northern Territories; Royal Commission on the West Indies	Baden-Powell, *Matabele War*; Conrad, *The Nigger of the 'Narcissus'*; Henty, *On the Irrawaddy*; Kingsley, *Travels in West Africa*; Kipling, 'Recessional'; Schreiner, *Trooper Peter Halkett*; Wyatt, 'Ethics of Empire'

1898	British victory at Omdurman; Fashoda incident; Curzon becomes Viceroy of India; Kowloon & Weihaiwei leased; Chamberlain's 5-Year Plan for the West Indies; Niger Convention with France	anon., *The Empire Reciter*; Kipling, *'Kitchener's School'*; Newbolt, *'The Island Race'*; Steevens, *With Kitchener to Khartoum*; Wells, *War of the Worlds*
1899	Anglo-French convention over Sudan; 2nd Anglo-Boer War (1899–1902); Dec: 'Black Week' of British defeats; Solomon Islands and Tonga annexed	Churchill, *The River War*; Hardy, *'Embarcation'*; Henley, *'Remonstrance'*; Kipling, *Stalky & Co.*; *'White Man's Burden'*; Newbolt, *The Island Race*; Swinburne, *'The Transvaal'*; Walton, *'Imperialism'*
1900	Relief of Ladysmith, Kimberley and Mafeking; Boxer Rebellion in China; Oct: Khaki election; First Pan-African Congress; *Daily Express* founded	Austin, *Songs of England*; Buchanan *'Voice of the Hooligan'*; Conan Doyle, *Great Boer War*; Conrad, *Lord Jim*; Cramb, *Reflections on Origins and Destiny of Imperial Britain*; Henley, *For England's Sake*; Hobson, *The War in South Africa*; Pearson, *National Life from the Standpoint of Science*
1901	Accession of Edward VII; Ashanti annexed; Commonwealth of	Buchanan, *Poetical Works*; Gooch, *Heart of the Empire*; Henty,

Australia; North-West Frontier Province created; Elgar, '*Pomp and Circumstance, March No. 1*'

With Buller in Natal; Hobson, *Psychology of Jingoism*; Kipling, *Kim*; Masterman, *Heart of Empire*; Rosebery, *Questions of Empire*

1902 Balfour Prime Minister; Anglo-Japanese Alliance; Colonial Conference; Peace of Vereeniging

Conrad, *The Heart of Darkness*; Davidson, '*Testament of an Empire Builder*'; Henty, *With Roberts to Pretoria*; *At the Point of a Bayonet*; *To Herat and Kabul*; Kipling, '*The Islanders*'; Mason, *The Four Feathers*; Watson, '*The Inexorable Law*'

1903 Chamberlain resigns as Colonial Secretary; Tariff Reform League; Empire Day implemented

Buchan, *The African Colony*; Henty, *With Kitchener in the Soudan*; Kipling, *Five Nations*; Watson, '*Rome and Another*'

1904 Anglo-French Entente settles problems in Egypt and Morocco

Conrad, *Nostromo*; Galsworthy, *The Island Pharisee*; Henty, *Through Three Campaigns*; Kipling, *Traffics & Discoveries*; Swinburne, *A Channel Passage*

1905 Bengal partitioned; Milner replaced in South Africa; Alberta & Saskatchewan created;

Haggard, *Ayesha*; Henty, *In the Hands of the Malays*; Lawson, *Cartoons in Rhyme and Line*

1906	Campbell-Bannerman Prime Minister	Buchan, *Lodge in the Wilderness*; Strang, *Samba*
1907	Anglo-Russian Convention; Imperial Conference	Mason, *The Broken Road*; Maugham, *The Explorer*; Twain, *King Leopold's Soliloquy*
1908	Asquith Prime Minister; Belgian state takes over control of the Congo from Leopold II; Boy Scouts founded; *Standard of Empire* founded	Baden-Powell, *Scouting for Boys*; Cromer, *Modern Egypt*; Curzon, 'The True Imperialism'; Newbolt, 'Clifton Chapel'
1909	Morley-Minto Reforms in India; Indian Councils Act; Kelantan, Trengganu, Kedah, Perlis under British protection	Conan Doyle, *The Crime of the Congo*; Vance, *The Bronze Bell*
1910	Union of South Africa formed	Buchan, *Prester John*; Cromer, *Ancient and Modern Imperialism*; Forster, *Howard's End*; Kipling, 'If'
1911	Agadir crisis; Imperial Conference; Delhi Durbar; Crystal Palace 'Dominions' Exhibition	Fletcher & Kipling, *School History of England*; Earl of Meath, *Essays on Duty and Discipline*; Wallace, *Sanders of the River*; Wells, *The New Machiavelli*
1912	Partition of Bengal revoked	Conan Doyle, *The Lost World*; Haggard, *Marie*; Perrin, *The Anglo-Indians*;

		Wallace, *The People of the River*
1913		Haggard, *Child of Storm*; Milner, *Nation and Empire*; Savi, *The Daughter-in-Law*; Woolf, *The Village in the Jungle*
1914	Aug: First World War begins; Resident in Johore; Cyprus annexed; Protectorate over Egypt	Burroughs, *Tarzan of the Apes*; Diver, *The Great Amulet*; Wallace, *Bosambo of the River*
1916	Lloyd George Prime Minister	Lenin, *Imperialism, the Highest Stage of Capitalism*
1917	Montagu declaration (India); Imperial War Conference	Haggard, *Finished*; Kipling, *A Diversity of Creatures*; Owen, 'Dulce et decorum est'
1919	Massacre at Amritsar; Government of India Act	Maugham, *Moon and Sixpence*; Newbolt, 'Drake's Drum'
1922	Bonar Law Prime Minister; Egypt granted nominal independence under King Fuad I; Irish Free State established	Forster, *Reflection of India: Too Late*; Lugard, *The Dual Mandate in British Tropical Africa*; Wallace, *Sandi, the Kingmaker*
1924	Empire Exhibition at Wembley	Forster, *A Passage to India*

A Guide to Reading

Primary Sources

Modern editions are listed whenever available:

Adderley, Charles Bowyer, *Review of 'The Colonial Policy of Lord John Russell's Administration' by Earl Grey, 1853; and of Subsequent Colonial Policy* (Edward Stanford, 1869)

anon., *The Empire Reciter for Platform, School and Home, with a Selection for Little Children* (Sunday School Union, 1898)

Ashe, Thomas (ed.), *The Table Talk and Omniana of Samuel Taylor Coleridge* (G. Bell & Sons, 1884)

Ashworth, James George, *Imperial Ben. A Jew d'Esprit* (Remington & Co., 1879)

Baden-Powell, Robert, *Scouting for Boys* (1908), (Penguin, 1990)

Ballantyne, Robert M., *The Coral Island* (1857), ed. J. S. Bratton (Oxford University Press, 1990)

—, *Six Months at the Cape* (J. Nisbet & Co., 1879)

Buchan, John, *The African Colony* (Blackwood & Sons, 1903)

—, *A Lodge in the Wilderness* (T. Nelson & Son, 1906)

—, *Prester John* (1910), ed. D. Daniell (Oxford University Press, 1994)

Bulwer-Lytton, Edward George Earle, *The Caxtons: A Family Picture*, 3 vols (W. Blackwood & Son, 1849)

Burke, Edmund, *Works of the Rt. Hon. Edmund Burke*, 16 vols, edited by Walker King & French Laurence (F. C. & J. Rivington, 1826)

Burroughs, Edgar Rice, *Tarzan of the Apes* (A. L. Burt & Co., 1914)

Buxton, Sir Thomas Fowell, *The African Slave Trade and its Remedy* (2nd edn, John Murray, 1840)

Carlyle, Thomas, *Chartism* (1839), (Holerth Library, No. 40, 1924)

Carlyle, Thomas, 'Occasional Discourse on the Nigger Question', *Fraser's Magazine* (December, 1849)

—, *Latter-Day Pamphlets No. IV: The New Downing Street* (1850), ed. M. K. Goldberg & J. P. Seigel (Canadian Federation for the Humanities, 1984)

Cary, Arthur Joyce Lunel, *A House of Children* (Michael Joseph, 1941)

—, *Britain and West Africa* (Longmans, Green, 1946)

Conrad, Joseph, *Almayer's Folly: A Story of an Eastern River* (1895), ed. J. Berthoud (Oxford University Press, 1992)

—, *An Outcast of the Islands* (1896), (Oxford University Press, 1992)

—, *Lord Jim* (1900), (Penguin, 1994)

—, *Heart of Darkness* (1902), (Penguin, 1994)

—, *Notes on Life and Letters* (J. M. Dent & Sons, 1921)

—, *Last Essays* (J. M. Dent & Sons, 1926)

— and Ford, Ford Madox, *The Inheritors: an Extravagant Story* (1901), (A. Sutton, 1991)

Cramb, John Adam, *Reflections on the Origins and Destiny of Imperial Britain* (Macmillan, 1900). Reprinted with additional material as *The Origins and Destiny of Imperial Britain* (John Murray, 1915)

Darwin, Charles, *On the Origins of Species by Means of Natural Selection*, 2 vols (1859), (Penguin, 1969)

—, *The Descent of Man and Selection in Relation to Sex*, 2 vols (1871), (Culture and Civilisation, Brussels, 1969)

Davidson, John, *The Testament of an Empire Builder* (Grant Richards, 1902)

Dilke, Sir Charles, *Greater Britain: A Record of Travel in English-Speaking Countries During 1866 and 1867* (Macmillan, 1868)

Disraeli, Benjamin, *Tancred*, 3 vols (Henry Colburn, 1847)

Diver, Maud, *The Singer Passes: An Indian Tapestry* (W. Blackwood & Sons, 1934)

Egerton, Hugh Edward (ed.), *Selected Speeches of Sir William Molesworth on Questions Relating to Colonial Policy* (John Murray, 1903)

Fletcher, Charles Robert Leslie, and Kipling, Rudyard, *A History of England* (Clarendon Press, 1911)

Forster, Edward Morgan, *Howards End* (1910), (Hodder, 1991)

—, *A Passage to India* (1924), ed. O. Stallybrass (Penguin, 1989)

—, *Abinger Harvest* (Edward Arnold & Co., 1936)

—, *The Hill of Devi: Being Letters From Dewas State Senior* (1953), (Penguin, 1983)

Fox, William, *A Brief History of the Wesleyan Missions on the Coast of Africa* (London, 1851)

Galsworthy, John, *The Island Pharisee* (William Heinemann, 1904)

Grey, Henry George, 3rd Earl, *The Colonial Policy of Lord John Russell's Administration*, 2 vols (Richard Bentley, 1853)

Haggard, Sir Henry Rider, *King Solomon's Mines* (1885), (Oxford University Press, 1989)

—, *Allan Quatermain* (1887), (Wordsworth, 1994)

—, *She* (1887), (Penguin, 1994)

—, *Nada the Lily* (1892), (Macdonald, 1949)

—, *Child of Storm* (1913), (Macdonald, 1952)

Henley, William Ernest, *Poems* (Macmillan, 1926)

Henty, George Alfred, *By Sheer Pluck: A Tale of the Ashanti War* (Blackie & Son, 1884)

—, *With Clive in India; or, The Beginnings of an Empire* (Blackie & Son, 1884)

—, *The Young Colonists: A Story of the Zulu and Boer Wars* (Blackie & Son, 1885)

—, *With Roberts to Pretoria: A Tale of the South African War* (Blackie & Son, 1902)

Hobson, John A., *The Psychology of Jingoism* (Grant Richards, 1901)

—, *Imperialism, A Study* (1902), (Unwin Hyman, 1988)

Huskisson, William, *Speeches of the Rt. Hon. William Huskisson*, 3 vols (London, 1831)

Kebbel, Thomas Edward, *Selected Speeches of the Late Earl of Beaconsfield*, 2 vols (Longmans, Green & Co., 1882)

Kipling, Rudyard, *In Black and White* (A. H. Wheeler & Co., 1888)

—, *Plain Tales from the Hills* (1888), (Penguin, 1994)

—, *Soldiers Three* (1888), (Penguin, 1993)

—, *The Light that Failed* (1890), (Macmillan, 1990)

—, *The Jungle Book* (1894) and *The Second Jungle Book* (1895), ed. W. W. Robson (Oxford University Press, 1992)

—, *Kim* (1901), ed. T. Royle (Everyman, 1994)

—, *The Definitive Edition of Rudyard Kipling's Verse* (Hodder & Stoughton, 1982). [*Complete Verse*, (K. Cathie, 1990)]

—, *Early Verse by Rudyard Kipling, 1879–1889: Unpublished, Uncollected and Rarely Collected Poems*, ed. A. Rutherford (Oxford University Press, 1992)

Knight, William Angus (ed.), *Rectorial Addresses delivered at the University of St Andrews, 1863–93* (A. & C. Black, 1894)

Knox, Robert, *The Races of Men: A Fragment* (Renshaw, 1850)

Lang, Andrew, *Essays in Little* (Whitefriars, 1891)

Lawson, Sir Wilfrid, *Cartoons in Rhyme and Line* (T. Fisher Unwin, 1905)

Lugard, Sir Frederick, *The Dual Mandate in British Tropical Africa* (W. Blackwood & Sons, 1922)

Marryat, Captain Frederick, *Masterman Ready*, 2 vols (Longman, Orme, Brown, Green & Longmans, 1841)

Maugham, William Somerset, *The Explorer* (Heinemann, 1907)

McCulloch, John Ramsay, *A Statistical Account of the British Empire*, 2 vols (London, 1837)

Meath, Reginald Brabazon, 2nd Earl of, 'Duty and discipline in the training of children' in *Essays on Duty and Discipline* (Cassell & Co., 1911)

Mill, John Stuart, *Principles of Political Economy* (1848), (Sir William Ashley, ed., Longmans, Green, 1909; reprinted Kelley, 1987)

—, *Autobiography* (1873), (new edn, Longmans, 1908)

Monk, William (ed.), *Dr. Livingstone's Cambridge Lectures* (Deighton, Bell, 1858)

Newbolt, Sir Henry, *Poems New and Old* (Murray, 1919)

Orwell, George, *Burmese Days* (1934), (Penguin, 1990)

—, *The Road to Wigan Pier* (1937), (Penguin, 1989)

—, *Collected Essays, Journalism and Letters, Vol. 1: An Age Like This, 1920–1940*, edited by S. Orwell & I. Angus (1968), (Penguin, 1993)

Owen, Sidney James, *A Selection from the Despatches and Other Papers of the Marquis of Wellesley during his Government in India* (Clarendon Press, 1877)

Pearson, Karl, *National Life from the Standpoint of Science* (A. & C. Black, 1900)

Roebuck, John A., *The Colonies of England* (Parker, 1849)

Rosebery, Archibald Philip Primrose, 5th Earl of, *Questions of Empire* (Arthur L. Humphreys, 1900)

Ruskin, John, *Lectures on Art* (1870), (George Allen, 1905)

Savi, Ethel Winifred, *The Daughter-in-Law* (Hurst & Blackett, 1913)

Seeley, Sir John Robert, *The Expansion of England: Two Courses of Lectures* (Macmillan, 1883)

Shaw, George Bernard, *The Man of Destiny* (1896), (Players Press, 1992)

Smith, Goldwin, *The Empire: A Series of Letters Published in the 'Daily News'* (Parker, 1863)

Southey, Robert, *Essays, Moral and Political*, 2 vols (London, 1832)

Spencer, Herbert, *Principles of Biology*, 2 vols (Williams & Norgate, 1865–7)

Stanley, Henry Morton, *How I Found Livingstone*, 2 vols (Sampson Low, 1872)

Stowe, Harriet Elizabeth Beecher, *Uncle Tom's Cabin, or Life Among the Lowly* (T. Bosworth, 1852)

Tennyson, Alfred, Lord, *The Poems of Tennyson*, edited by Christopher Ricks, 3 vols (Longmans, 1987)

Trevelyan, Sir George Otto, *Life and Letters of Macaulay*, 2 vols (1876), (Oxford University Press, 1932)

Trollope, Anthony, *The West Indies and the Spanish Main* (1859), (A. Sutton, 1985)

—, *North America*, 2 vols (1862), (A. Sutton, 1987)

—, *Australia and New Zealand*, 2 vols (1873), (A. Sutton, 1987)

—, *South Africa*, 2 vols (1878), (A. Sutton, 1987)

Vance, Louis Joseph, *The Bronze Bell* (Grant Richards, 1909)

Wallace, R. H. Edgar, *Sanders of the River* (1911), (Ward Lock, 1933)

Watson, Sir William, *The Poems of Sir William Watson, 1878–1935*, 2 vols (1905), (G. G. Harrap, 1936)

Welldon, James Edward Cowell, 'The Early Training of Boys into Citizenship' in *Essays on Duty and Discipline* (Cassell & Co., 1910)

Wilberforce, William, *An Appeal to the Religion, Justice, and Humanity of the Inhabitants of the British Empire, In Behalf of the Negro Slaves in the West Indies* (London, 1823)

Woolf, Leonard Sidney, *Growing: An Autobiography of the Years 1904–1911* (Hogarth Press, 1961)

Wordsworth, William, *The Excursion* (Longman & Co., 1814)

Young, George Malcolm (ed.), *Macaulay: Prose and Poetry* (1967), (Hart-Davis, 1970)

Secondary Sources, Introductory

Bennett, George (ed.), *The Concept of Empire: Burke to Attlee, 1774–1947* (Adam & Charles Black, 2nd edn, 1967)

Brantlinger, Patrick, *Rule of Darkness: British Literature and Imperialism, 1830–1914* (Cornell University Press, 1988)

Eldridge, Colin C., *Victorian Imperialism* (Hodder & Stoughton, 1978)

Green, Martin, *Dreams of Adventure, Deeds of Empire* (Routledge & Kegan Paul, 1980)

MacKenzie, John M., *Propaganda and Empire: The Manipulation of British Public Opinion, 1880–1960* (Manchester University Press, 1984)

McDonough, Frank, *The British Empire, 1815–1914* (Hodder & Stoughton, 1994)

Morris, Jan, *The Spectacle of Empire: Style, Effect and the Pax Britannica* (Faber & Faber, 1982)

Said, Edward W., *Culture and Imperialism* (Chatto & Windus, 1993)

Sandison, Alan, *The Wheel of Empire: A Study of the Imperial Idea in the Late Nineteenth and Early Twentieth-Century Fiction* (Macmillan, 1967)

Further Reading 1

Bivona, Daniel, *Desire and Contradiction: Imperial Visions and Domestic Debates in Victorian Literature* (Manchester University Press, 1990)

Bolt, Christine A., *Victorian Attitudes to Race* (Routledge & Kegan Paul, 1971)

Bristow, Joseph J., *Empire Boys: Adventures in a Man's World* (Harper Collins Academic, 1991)

Chakravarty, Suhash, *The Raj Syndrome: A Study in Imperial Perceptions* (Chanakya Publications, 1989)

Dabydeen, David, *The Black Presence in English Literature* (Manchester University Press, 1985)

Eldridge, Colin C. (ed.), *British Imperialism in the Nineteenth Century* (Macmillan, 1984)

Field, H. John, *Toward a Programme of Imperial Life: The British Empire at the Turn of the Century* (Clio, 1982)

Gidley, Mick, *Representing Others: White Views of Indigenous Peoples* (Exeter University Press, 1992)

Goonetilleke, D. C. R. A., *Developing Countries in British Fiction* (Macmillan, 1977)

—, *Images of the Raj: South Asia in the Literature of Empire* (Macmillan, 1988)

Greenberger, Allen J., *The British Image of India: A Study in the Literature of Imperialism, 1880–1960* (Oxford University Press, 1969)

Hutchins, Francis G., *The Illusion of Permanence: British Imperialism in India* (Princeton University Press, 1967)

Inden, Ronald, *Imagining India* (Blackwell, 1990)

Islam, Shamsul, *Chronicles of the Raj: A Study of the Literary Reaction to the Imperial Idea Towards the End of the Raj* (Macmillan, 1979)

Killam, G. D., *Africa in English Fiction, 1874–1939* (Ibadan University Press, 1968)

Koebner, Richard, and Schmidt, Helmut D., *Imperialism: the Story and Significance of a Political Word, 1840–1960* (Cambridge University Press, 1964)

MacDonald, Robert H., *The Language of Empire* (Manchester University Press, 1994)

MacKenzie, John M. (ed.), *Imperialism and Popular Culture* (Manchester University Press, 1985)

—, (ed.), *Popular Imperialism and the Military* (Manchester University Press, 1992)

Mahood, Molly M., *The Colonial Encounter: A Reading of Six Novels* (Collings, 1977)

Mangan, James A., *'Benefits Bestowed'? Education and British Imperialism* (Manchester University Press, 1988)

—, *Making Imperial Mentalities: Socialisation and British Imperialism* (Manchester University Press, 1990)

Meyers, Jeffery, *Fiction and the Colonial Experience* (Boydell, 1972)

Parry, Benita, *Delusions and Discoveries: Studies on India in the British Imagination, 1880–1930* (Allen & Unwin, 1972)

Pieterse, Jan Nederveen, *White on Black: Images of Africa and Blacks in Western Popular Culture* (Yale University Press, 1992)

Ray, Gordon N., *Thackeray: The Age of Wisdom* (Oxford University Press, 1958)

Richards, Jeffery (ed.), *Imperialism and Juvenile Literature* (Manchester University Press, 1988)

Ridley, Hugh, *Images of Imperial Rule* (Croom Helm, 1983)

Street, Brian V., *The Savage in Literature: Representations of Primitive Society in English Fiction, 1858–1920* (Routledge & Kegan Paul, 1975)

Suleri, Sara, *The Rhetoric of English India* (Chicago University Press, 1993)

Viswanathan, Gauri, *Masks of Conquest: Literary Study and British Rule in India* (Faber, 1990)

Further Reading 2

Arnold, Guy, *Held Fast for England: G. A. Henty, Imperialist Boys' Writer* (H. Hamilton, 1980)

Bradbury, Malcolm, *E.M. Forster – 'A Passage to India': A Casebook* (Macmillan, 1970)

Burden, Robert, *Heart of Darkness* (Macmillan, 1991)

Crowell, Norton B., *Alfred Austin: Victorian* (Weidenfeld & Nicholson, 1955)

Das, G. K., *E. M. Forster's India* (Macmillan, 1977)

Etherington, Norman, *Rider Haggard* (Twayne, 1984)

Gilbert, Elliot Lewis (ed.), *Kipling and the Critics* (Owen, 1965)

Gross, John (ed.), *Rudyard Kipling. The Man, his Work, and his World* (Weidenfeld & Nicholson, 1972)

Islam, Shamsul, *Kipling's Law: A Study of His Philosophy of Life* (Macmillan, 1975)

Jamiluddin, K., *The Tropic Sun: Rudyard Kipling and the Raj* (Lucknow University, 1974)

Katz, Wendy R., *Rider Haggard and the Fiction of Empire: A Critical Study of British Imperial Fiction* (Cambridge University Press, 1987)

Keating, Peter, *Kipling the Poet* (Secker & Warburg, 1994)

Kimborough, R. (ed.), *Heart of Darkness: An Authoritative Text, Backgrounds and Sources, Criticism* (W. W. Norton, 3rd edn, 1988)

Knaplund, Paul, *Gladstone and Britain's Imperial Policy* (Allen & Unwin, 1927)

Lane, Margaret, *Edgar Wallace: The Biography of a Phenomenon* (William Heinemann, 1938)

Langer, William Leonard, *The Diplomacy of Imperialism, 1890–1902* (Alfred A. Knopf, 1965)

Lee, Robert F., *Conrad's Colonialism* (Mouton, 1969)

Lownie, Andrew, *John Buchan: the Presbyterian Cavalier* (Constable, 1995)

Maugham, William Somerset, *A Choice of Kipling's Prose* (Macmillan, 1952)

McClure, John A., *Kipling and Conrad: The Colonial Fiction* (Harvard University Press, 1981)

Monkshood, G. F., *Rudyard Kipling, The Man and his Work – An Attempt at Appreciation* (Greening & Co., 1902)

Murfin, Ross C., *Conrad Revisited: Essays for the Eighties* (Alabama University Press, 1985)

—, *Heart of Darkness: A Case Study in Contemporary Criticism* (St Martin's Press, 1989)

Orel, Harold (ed.), *Critical Essays on Rudyard Kipling* (G. K. Hall, 1989)

Parry, Ann, *The Poetry of Rudyard Kipling: Rousing the Nation* (Open University Press, 1992)

Parry, Benita, *Conrad and Imperialism: Ideological Boundaries and Visionary Frontiers* (Macmillan, 1983)

Pocock, Tom, *Rider Haggard and the Lost Empire* (Weidenfeld & Nicholson, 1993)

Quayle, Eric, *Ballantyne the Brave: A Victorian Writer and His Family* (Rupert Hart-Davis, 1967)

Pafford, Mark, *Kipling's Indian Fiction* (Macmillan, 1989)

Rutherford, Andrew (ed.), *Kipling's Mind and Art* (Oliver & Boyd, 1964)

Shahane, V. A. (ed.), *Perspectives on E. M. Forster's 'A Passage to India': A Collection of Critical Essays* (Barnes & Noble, 1968)

Shahane, V. A. (ed.), *Focus on Forster's 'A Passage to India': Indian Essays in Criticism* (Orient Longman, 1972)

Sherry, Norman, *Conrad's Eastern World* (Cambridge University Press, 1966)

Sinfield, Alan, *Alfred Tennyson* (Blackwell, 1986)

Spittles, Brian, *Joseph Conrad: Text and Context* (Macmillan Educational, 1992)

Sullivan, Zahreh T., *Narratives of Empire: the Fictions of Rudyard Kipling* (Cambridge University Press, 1993)

White, Andrea, *Joseph Conrad and the Adventure Tradition: Constructing and Deconstructing the Imperial Subject* (Cambridge University Press, 1993)

Zins, Henryk, *Joseph Conrad and Africa* (Kenya Literature Bureau, 1982)

Other Books Quoted in the Text

Attlee, Clement Richard, *Empire into Commonwealth* (Oxford University Press, 1961)

Darwin, Bernard Richard Meirion, *The English Public School* (Longmans, Green, 1929)

Dicey, Albert Venn, *Lectures on the Relation between Law and Public Opinion in England During the Nineteenth Century* (2nd edn, Macmillan, 1914)

Gandhi, Mohandas Karamchand, *The Collected Works of Mahatma Gandhi*, 90 vols (Publications Division of the Government of India, 1958–84)

Gardiner, Alfred George, *Life of Sir William Harcourt*, 2 vols (Constable, 1923)

Headlam, Cecil (ed.), *The Milner Papers: South Africa. Vol. II: 1895–1905*, 2 vols (Cassell, 1933)

Hume, Andrew Hamilton, *Life of Edward John Eyre* (Richard Bentley, 1867)

James, Robert Rhodes (ed.), *Winston S. Churchill: His Complete Speeches*, 8 vols (Chelsea House Publishers, 1974)

Kaunda, Kenneth, *Zambia Shall Be Free* (Heinemann, 1962)

Lawrence, Sir Walter Roper, *The India We Served* (Cassell, 1928)

Long, Edward, *The History of Jamaica*, 3 vols (J. T. Lowndes, 1774)

MacKenzie, Jeanne, and MacKenzie, Norman (eds), *The Diary of Beatrice Webb*, 4 vols (Harvard University Press, 1983)

Magnus, Philip, *Gladstone, a Biography* (John Murray, 1954)

Masterman, Charles Frederick Gurney, *In Peril of Change* (T. Fisher Unwin, 1905)

Michell, Lewis, *The Life of the Rt. Hon. Cecil Rhodes*, 2 vols (Edward Arnold, 1910)

Nehru, Jawaharlal, *Autobiography* (1936), (Oxford University Press, 1991)

Oliver, Roland Anthony, *Sir Harry Johnston and the Scramble for Africa* (Chatto & Windus, 1957)

Panikkar, K. M., *Asia and Western Dominance; A Survey of the Vasco Da Gama Epoch of Asian History, 1498–1945* (Allen & Unwin, 1953)

Raleigh, Sir Thomas, *Lord Curzon in India* (Macmillan, 1906)

Roberts, R., *The Classic Slum* (Manchester University Press, 1971)

Roeykens, Aug., *Léopold II et la conférence géographique de Bruxelles, 1876* (Académie Royale des Sciences Coloniales, 1956)

Scott, Paul, *The Day of the Scorpion* (William Heinemann, 1968)

Semmel, Bernard, *The Governor Eyre Controversy* (McGibbon & Kee, 1962)

Stratford, Esmé Cecil Wingfield-, *The Foundations of British Patriotism* (Routledge & Sons, 1940)

Index